Soul Sight

Projections of Consciousness
and
Out of Body Epiphanies

Lulu, Inc.

First published 2008

Copyright © Mary E. Barton 2008

ISBN 978-0-557-02163-5 (pbk.): $20.00

Printed and bound in the United States of America

by Lulu, Inc.

www.Lulu.com

To Robert H. Barton, who for many years created a world of joy and emotional nourishment for me; to my son, Brian Barton, who demonstrates that unconditional love exists; and to all courageous travelers of unknown paths.

mystical moments
answer to one question:
more questions!

Acknowledgements

This book would not be complete without acknowledging a few special people. Thank you, Suzanne DeLisle and Richard Kendall, for your encouragement and help ages past. Thank you, George O'Keefe, for our fascinating mental connection. I would also like to express my eternal thanks to Seth, Jane Roberts and Robert F. Butts. My world would not be the wonderful, magical place it is except for you.

Table of Contents

Preface

To bare one's soul is never easy. If I were asked, "What of your life, other than loved ones, do you hold most sacred? What of your life do you most value?" I would hand them this book and say, quite simply, "This."

It still was not an easy decision to write this book. I kept vacillating between yes and no. I had a lovely life and other interests; I didn't need to do this. Everyone who wanted to would find his own path ... but memories of my own frustrations nagged at me. I remember being annoyed by metaphysical writers who refused to tell, other than a few anecdotes, *what* they were experiencing. When you are going through what I did, you crave *all* the information you can find.

Finally, after weeks of debating the issue, I fervently wished I could have the advice of someone whom I admired for both his writing ability and his inspiration to the world: author Richard Bach.

When I realized what I was doing, my egotistical, left-brained, logical, doubting self immediately thought, "Yeah, right. And moonbeams will be purple tonight," and dismissed the thought. A few minutes later, I received an impulse to visit the library. Since I am an avid reader, I had little reluctance to follow that kind of advice, and immediately drove to the library.

While browsing through the biographies section, I was surprised to find an unfamiliar book called

Above the Clouds by Jonathan Bach. It appeared to be written by the father of the author of one of my favorite books, *Illusions*. I thought it might be interesting, so I checked it out.

Well, as the saying goes, miracles never cease. It was *not* written by Richard Bach's father, but by his son, who, in the context of his book, was trying to decide whether or not to write a revealing book about his relationship with his father, Richard. Just what *I* was trying to do - write a revealing book about myself!

They say nothing ever happens by chance.

Richard Bach's advice to his son and to me?

"Write your book. Write every word."

So, here it is.

Introduction

Traveling through intricate tunnels to reach this virtual haven of peace, abundance and natural beauty, I knew I had been here before. Though I couldn't consciously recall when I had been here, some part of my soul recognized and resonated with this out-of-body location and I immediately felt welcome. Undulating hills alive with greenery covered the countryside as far as the eye could see. In this ancestral landscape, each home had its own hill enabling each resident to have plenty of privacy. I say this, yet there was no evidence of man-made abodes to interrupt the soul-soothing natural beauty. Nature and man cooperated in some indescribable fashion that nourished and fulfilled the needs of the consciousnesses of both nature and man.

In a quaint village nearby, I walked through the cobblestone streets marveling at all I saw. Old world charm graced the gray stone business structures. Colorful signs describing the wares or function of each business swayed above my head. I came upon natural plantings of great beauty in the courtyards of some of the businesses; the peace and harmony of the commercial section enthralled me.

As I inspected some particularly interesting fruit trees, I suddenly noticed I had a companion. She was so unobtrusive and her presence felt so familiar, she could have been a part of myself. She was as peacefully composed as the rest of the environment. For this reason, I don't know how long she was actually beside me. I had been so caught up with the beauty of the place, she could have been there for centuries. She was a slightly plump, white-haired, elderly woman.

She informed me that the unique, other-worldly tree specie I was gazing at was a bread tree. You just picked the bread off the tree like fruit. When she emptied some of the powdered bread fruit into my hand from a drawstring medicine bag and encouraged me to try it, the thought entered my mind that this bread would not have the wonderful aroma of baking bread. With some hesitation I tasted the fruit and was overcome by the flavor. It was delicious! Unbelievably spectacular! Exclaiming in delight, I became quite excited. I wanted to bring some back home with me. I knew that people would love it!

I thought the fruit could be of great benefit to the world. I began thinking of the marketing possibilities. How would I transport the trees? How would I get the word out to people? Who would hear of it? Where would they find it? Then I caught myself, stopped my out-of-body ruminations, looked at my companion and wondered: *Who is this woman? Who is this woman in this amazing world with these amazing trees?*

For the first time in my out-of-body travels, I was communicating with someone more powerful than I; someone who could influence me beyond anything I had thus far encountered. At this point, in response to my unspoken questions, **an image was placed in my mind**. Due to our family habit of sharing entertainment regardless of age or interest, the image was one I recognized. It was a picture of the Disney cartoon character, The Friendly Giant. Incongruous as this sounds, I didn't have time to question the significance of the image, because transmitted with the image was a built-in comprehension, a depth of knowledge that overwhelmed me. I was immediately awed to the furthest reaches of my being. Not because of the recognizable image, but because I understood.

She was an ANIMATOR. A BRINGER OF THINGS TO LIFE. SHE MADE LIFE LIVE.

Impressed beyond description, I was immediately transported back to my physical body. Thrilled to the core of my soul, I ... but I digress, and I'm far ahead of my story. My out-of-body journeys began in quite another fashion ...

Soul Sight

Projections of Consciousness
and
Out of Body Epiphanies

Mary E. Barton

The Visitor

*In the same way in the midst of life, you dwell with
so-called ghosts and apparitions, and for that matter
you yourselves appear as apparitions to others,
particularly when you send strong thought-forms of
yourself from the sleep state, or even when
unconsciously you travel out of your body.*

Seth, Seth Speaks, Session 539

Rich earth smells mingled with others
emanating from the gardening tools, books,
and miscellaneous household goods stored
around the perimeter of the bed. Tim, my new
husband, closed the door to the storeroom, our
temporary bedroom, shutting out the darkness of the
night air. We undressed quietly, conversation spent,
as the rustling of clothes, the whir of the deep-
freezer, and the crackling of the propane heater filled
the void of our silence. Climbing into bed, I was in a
highly optimistic mood, despite the less than ideal
physical situation in which I found myself.

I was a newlywed of two months, and had
recently reunited with my husband after a brief
separation. We had just moved to New Mexico from

Los Angeles, and were staying with his parents until we could find an apartment of our own. Tim was an elementary school history teacher, and an avid, talented Rock-and-Roll musician.

I was nineteen, in love, living with virtual strangers, far from my immediate family. Ours had been a whirlwind relationship which resulted in a quick marriage after a brief engagement. Tensions abated; I felt wonderful after all of the decisions, plans, and move had been carried out.

I was now about to begin a life in a desert land completely dissimilar to the verdant farmland where I had been reared. En route to this area, I had been appalled by the desolation before me. Deadened by winter, the desert vegetation held no charm, the worn adobe houses leaked despair, the crusty arroyos were witnesses to infertile conditions. Though shocked by the barrenness of the area, the ignorance of youth and the promise of love enticed me to ignore my misgivings. Surely life would be good. I was with my husband, after all. What could go wrong? I climbed into bed, settled under the blankets and relaxed. Tim soon joined me and switched off the bedside lamp. The blackness of the room was slightly relieved by the glow of the fire seen through the vents in the propane heater.

I closed my eyes, anticipating sleep, when suddenly, I was startled by the sight of an American Indian standing beside our bed! He was a young brave, approximately eighteen years old, thin, with jet-black hair flowing loose beneath his headband.

4

Chest bare, he was wrapped in a breechcloth, holding an upraised tomahawk in one hand.

I physically jerked back in fright and let out an involuntary exclamation. A bewildered Tim asked, "What's wrong?"

"Turn on the light," I said in a panic. Tim quickly did so and turned to look at me. "What's wrong?" he repeated.

I raised myself on my arms as I peered around the room looking for the intruder. "There was an Indian standing beside our bed." My heart pounded in fright.

"What?!!"

"There was an Indian standing right there," I said, pointing to where the young man had been standing, too shocked to go into detail.

My husband gave me an incredulous look. "Are you sure?" he asked, looking around. There were no nooks or crannies in which someone could hide.

I answered with an emphatic, "Yes, he was right there! Good Grief, what on earth was it?"

"Maybe it was just a dream ..." he said, charitably.

Totally shaken, I replied with certainty, "It wasn't a dream, for Pete's sake, I wasn't even asleep yet!"

Tim looked around, still not seeing anything, came to his own conclusion, and said, "Well, it's not here now. Let's get some sleep."

"Couldn't we leave the light on for a while?" I asked, not wanting to face the darkness and what might be there. Acting like laser beams, my eyes

5

pierced every corner, every shadow of the apparently hostile room.

"No, what would my parents think?" his voice thick with exasperation and disdain. "There's nothing here. Just go to sleep. I have to work in the morning." Disgruntled by the disturbance, he abruptly turned off the light and rolled over. Too upset to take umbrage at his irritability, I lay there, tense, eyes open, staring about the dark room. Each rustle of the night sounds had me mentally seeking the reason for it.

Never having experienced anything like this before, my mind raced. What had it been? It obviously hadn't been three-dimensional. No one had physically been in the room with us, thank God, yet, it wasn't a dream. I knew it wasn't. I had still been awake, albeit, very relaxed.

Fear crept through me as I thought about the possibility that it might have been a ghost. I immediately discarded the idea. Ghosts didn't exist. At least, I thought they didn't. The only ghosts I had ever heard of were in Fright Night stories fabricated to tingle childish spines, or the other extreme, religious "ghosts," to neither of which I gave much credence.

A spontaneous hallucination was a possibility, but my sanity was one thing in which I had complete confidence. My mind was as sharp and clear as it could possibly be. It was underused at times, but, still, fine-tuned. I don't know how long I lay there contemplating my plight. Nature mercifully came to the rescue as I ran out of ideas and fell into the blessed unconscious state of sleep.

New Memory

*You cannot examine reality without examining
yourself, in other words. You cannot hold encounters
with All That Is apart from yourself, and you cannot
use "truth." It cannot be manipulated. Whoever thinks
he is manipulating truth is manipulating himself. You
<u>are</u> truth. Then discover yourself.*

Seth, Seth Speaks, *Session 596*

The next evening, perplexed by what I had seen and curious if my in-laws had ever seen anything similar in that room, I told them what had happened. They exchanged knowing glances and asked whether I had ever experienced anything similar before. I opened my mouth to answer confidently, "No, I hadn't," when an internal energy clicked into place and a scene appeared in my mind.

I was lying on the third or fourth step of the bare wood stairs leading to the basement of our home in the fertile Red River Valley of North Dakota. My lithe, five-year-old body maintained a delicate balance on the banister-free, open-to-the-room-below stairs that abutted the cement-block wall of the basement.

Alone, listening to the music waft by me from a television program the rest of the family was watching in another room, I was being brave.

I was staring into the deep, dark, seemingly infinite pit of the basement. The inky blackness was a challenge, a challenge to which only a five-year-old mind could succumb. Who knew what creatures one could find there? Who knew what lived there when the lights were out? I was following my quest of childish titillation when it happened.

A window in space and time opened.

Before me, women in floor-length, old-fashioned dresses, and men in long-sleeved shirts, or buttoned-almost-to-the-chin staid suits, were dancing in a rustic setting. I watched in delight as they stepped to and fro, circling each other, while the women's skirts flowed gracefully around their legs.

There were at least seven people that I could see at the frontier party, most of whom were paired in a line facing each other, tapping their toes and swaying to a rhythm. It was a lively, happy gathering. The scene was directly below me, but since there was more of the room to the right, I strained my head over the edge of the stairs to look in that direction. Doing so, I slipped from my precarious perch and tumbled down the stairs.

Over and over I turned, each encounter with an unrelenting step reminded me that I, at least, was physical. I hit the hard cement floor, tightly closed my eyes, and curled into the fetal position. I was scared now, and not about to move for anything. My cries of pain and surprise, plus the unexpected thumps down the stairs, brought exclamations from the living room, from which my older brother was

9

dispatched to see what had happened. He switched on the light, chiding me for my carelessness, and carried me up the stairs.

Placed before my mother, I immediately flung myself into her comforting arms. Once I had calmed down and she had ascertained that there were no serious injuries, she asked me in her best 'let's learn something from this' tone of voice, "What on earth were you doing on the stairs to begin with?"

In my complete innocence, I told her, "I was watching the dancers."

Every face in the room registered a shocked expression. My mother, surprised and unwittingly playing the straight-man, said, "What dancers?"

"The ones downstairs," I answered, matter-of-factly. "There were women in pretty, long dresses ..."

My devout, Roman Catholic mother, a good woman in every sense of the word, confronted by the inexplicable, knowing there were no strangers in her basement, responded in an astonished and brusque, "Have you lost your mind?!"

I drew back in shock as if I had been physically struck in the face. She didn't believe me. But there had been people there! I wasn't lying. Certain of what I had seen, I immediately tried to defend myself. "There were dancers there! They were right downstairs. The men were dressed in ..."

My mother stared at me, trying to comprehend what I was telling her. When she couldn't, she let out a sigh of disgust. My brothers and sisters started to snicker and laugh. I was in trouble for a change, not they. The more I tried to explain myself, the more I was derided.

My mother, not knowing what to do since nothing like this existed in her belief system, interrupted my explanations with her conclusion: "That is the most ridiculous thing I have ever heard of. You must have hit your head falling down the stairs." Then, pushing me away from her, she immediately changed the subject, "Isn't it about time you kids went to bed?"

Everyone groaned and started to argue, but mom insisted, and we all began our nightly get-ready-for-bed rituals.

I was hurt and confused by everyone's reaction. I knew what I had seen. I had seen dancers. I was not stupid; I learned quickly. If what I saw was not apparent nor acceptable to others, then I would no longer tell anyone of my visions.

"Isn't that strange," I commented to my in-laws after the new memory expanded into my consciousness and I explained to them what I had seen. "I don't remember that occurrence. There is the memory, but I don't remember experiencing it! It's like it was just placed there this moment! How can that be?" I sat there nonplussed. What was going on?

Prediction

When you understand the nature of reality, then you realize that predictions of future events are basically meaningless. You can predict some events and they can occur, but you create the future in every moment.

Seth, Seth Speaks, *Appendix*

Hal set down his coffee cup and said, "Maybe it's time we went over your astrology chart." My father-in-law, an intelligent, gentle man, much harassed by his own highly critical mother-in-law, was an amateur astrologer who had acquired my natal information from me when Tim and I first announced our engagement. "Let's go out to the storeroom."

As Tim began to rise along with us, Hal interrupted him with, "No, astrology is personal. You can't hear this, Tim." I looked at Hal in surprise and said, "I don't mind if he hears." But Hal was adamant, so the two of us left the mobile home together. I was excited and curious. I had no knowledge of astrology other than what I had read in daily newspaper horoscopes.

Hal sat across from me. A large chart and notes

lay on the table between us. For a few minutes he looked at the huge chart with its large circle, lines intersecting it and strange symbols within it, before he exhaled a deep sigh.

I immediately reacted with concern, "There isn't anything wrong, is there?"

"No, no. It's just that this won't be easy. According to the stars, you are a Cancer and Tim is a Sagittarius. Cancer is a water sign and Sagittarius is a fire sign. Which means you may not be very compatible."

I was startled, to say the least, as Hal continued. "In fact, the only reason I can see why the two of you even got together was because according to your birth time, you have a 29 Scorpio/0 Sagittarius ascendant. This is on the Cusp of Scorpio/ Sagittarius. So you may be able to make it." I sat further back in my chair. I definitely did not like the sound of that.

"Let's begin with you. You have a very complex personality. You will have characteristics of both the sign Scorpio and the sign Sagittarius, and they are as different as daylight and dark. Scorpio is deeply sensitive, keeps it all bottled up, does not cry a lot, does not complain a lot. Sagittarians *can* be very sensitive, but they are a communication sign whose members get it all out in the open ..."

"You see, you have three personal rulers. Mars and Pluto co-rule the sign Scorpio, and Jupiter rules the sign of Sagittarius, all of which combine to make you a very complex individual. You are not a simple soul. Nor will you react to the world in a simple way."

My mind strained as it tried to comprehend the foreign jargon.

"Let me put it this way: Scorpio functions on the emotional level and Sagittarius expresses itself on an intellectual level. So you are a combination of these two things, and it really is pretty remarkable ..." he said, with some surprise.

"Your personal ruler Jupiter, you see, and the sign Sagittarius are all involved with higher education, the development of the higher mind, higher philosophies, a highly developed religious sense, all those good things."

"But then, Mars and Pluto are not as easy to deal with as Jupiter. Mars is almost as serious as Pluto, but not quite, and they are very spiritually oriented, very philosophically oriented. They are like the Hermit, the Seeker after the Truth, the secrets that we don't know on this plane of existence. Now, two of your rulers, the two most important, Pluto and Jupiter, are fire signs. The fire signs have to do with spiritual development. So again, we have this tremendous, uncanny influence concerning spiritual development."

I sat there in silence, not knowing what to say. *What was he talking about?* I had no interest in religion or philosophy, I had no profound faith, and I was definitely not a church-goer.

Hal continued, "You have Virgo on the mid-heaven, and that sign is ruled by Mercury which rules the written or spoken word. You have Neptune in the 10th House which is indicative of psychic ability. You are so sensitive to other people that virtually you can read their minds. You know things about them that you have no accountable way of knowing, and you can be very helpful to them because of this."

An incredulous smile crept over my face. Could people do that? I had no desire to read anyone's mind. This was all so strange!

"Now overall, your chart balances out. You have the Sun, Venus, and Uranus in Cancer which gives it quite a lot of importance. It is self-activating, self-motivating. You don't want to be told to do something. You see what needs to be done and you do it." I certainly had to agree with that. I hated to be ordered around, but I had always thought it was a reaction to my domineering father.

"Cancer is a nurturing sign, and you tend to take care of all who come in contact with you. Family is important to you."

As Hal paused to catch his breath, I finally had the chance to ask a question, "What does it say about Tim and me?"

Hal cleared his throat. "You have 29 Taurus on the 7th Cusp, and this is ruled by a group of stars known as the Pleiades. You will have some problems, but if you work together to overcome these problems, you can make a success of the marriage." Looking down, Hal nervously fingered his notes.

"There are some indications that you will leave Tim for an older man in about five years."

"What?!" I exclaimed, practically leaping from my seat in total astonishment. I had no intention of leaving Tim! I loved him.

"But it does not have to work out that way." Hal rushed on. "These are only probabilities. You decide. You choose what will ultimately be."

I was rather incensed by the idea that I, this person deeply in love, newly married, might leave my husband. I thought to myself, "That is ridiculous!" when another question came to mind. "What about children? Does it show ..."

"There is no indication of children, but I only carried this out for about five years."

Well, that was that. What he said was preposterous. I wanted children and would not be leaving my husband for any older man. Just the other day I had given Tim my blessing that he could pursue his musical career for five years before we started a family. We had plans. Furthermore, I had no psychic abilities - whatever they were. He was obviously wrong. Keeping my opinions to myself, I politely thanked Hal and we went back in with the others. Tim looked at me curiously from his chair by the kitchen table. I wondered what his dad had told *him*. We never discussed it. But now I understood why Hal didn't want Tim to hear what was revealed. He must be wrong though, I thought, I married for life. Astrology, apparently, did not work.

Symptoms

*You are truly multi-dimensional personalities, as I
have said before. At some point in your development
you will become more and more aware of the true
nature of your identity.*

Seth, Seth Speaks, *Appendix*

Work at the bank was slow that day. No
angry customers came in to reconcile
their overdrawn accounts. None came
in to argue about bounced checks. Few even came in
to open their safe deposit boxes, so, I sat going
through a huge 3x5 account card file.

Hundreds of cards were in the file. The computer
listing I held was the Closed Account printout. Each
account on the list had a corresponding card in the
file which needed to be pulled. No one had done this
task in years, and on quiet days, I would find and
pull these cards. I would also add all New Account
cards to this catalogue.

It was monotonous, mindless work, but it was a
job, and one I did frequently between major paydays.
I had been working for a while, when I noticed it.

Invariably, wherever I placed my hands, they would be in the correct position! That is, without even trying, my fingers would be on the right card, or space, I needed.

Pleasantly surprised, and curious, I checked it out. I placed my hands on the cards, separated them with my fingers, glanced at the name to be extracted, and there was the card I needed. It was no coincidence. It happened again, and again, and again. Every time I touched the cards. I was smiling to myself when my boss passed by. "I didn't know filing cards could be so entertaining," he commented.

I laughed, embarrassed, and said, "Oh, it's just so funny. Every time I need a card or space, without actually looking, my fingers are right where they need to be: on the card or on the space. It's quite bizarre."

"Really?" he said with a smile, "Well, consider yourself lucky. I'm sure it makes the job a lot easier."

As he continued on his way, I grinned again as a thought entered my mind. Psychic fingers. I have psychic fingers. Nothing *else* about me appeared to be psychic, but I guess I'll take what I can get. Being psychic, I found, meant having extrasensory perception or telepathic abilities.

Ever since Hal's predictions, my Indian "ghost," and my spontaneously recalled new memory of the childhood experience, my curiosity propelled me into the study of alternate thought.

I ordered another astrology reading from a different source, but the results came back totally dissimilar to what Hal had told me due, I discovered, to the use of the incorrect birth time. I decided the results were unreliable, and looked into numerology. Numerology texts were general descriptions concerning character traits. All very interesting, but they held no information that I could find to explain my mysterious experiences. Coming across some material on Edgar Cayce, the so-called Sleeping Prophet, I was immediately intrigued.

Here was a man who, while in trance, was able to diagnose illnesses and cure people he didn't know, through being told by something called his Spirit Guides what the problems were and the solutions to those problems. It was all well-documented and very convincing. What surprised me more than anything, even the healings, were the implications that spiritual beings actually existed and helped man. It appeared it wasn't all fairy tales or wishful thinking, as I had previously judged it to be.

If that were the case, was my Indian brave also a spiritual being? If he was, then why did he contact me? He certainly had looked real enough! Or was he a symbol, albeit a very intimidating one, telling me to be courageous in my new life? Did symbols just appear out of thin air, while you were totally conscious? Not that I knew of, but whether the Indian brave was a spirit or a symbol, this still didn't tell me what the frontier party signified. It also didn't tell me why I had no prior memory of the party before I told my in-laws of the Indian brave. Why did I *now* have a complete memory of it, with history, repercussions and sense phenomena?

Investigating further, I found the most revolutionary, intriguing, and scary ideas I ever encountered from the author Jane Roberts and an energy personality essence called Seth. Their book, *Seth Speaks*, was written by Seth while Jane was in trance. This spiritual being stated emphatically that Consciousness creates form, individually and en masse. According to him, man is quite naturally telepathic and clairvoyant, and can learn to change his *physical* environment by learning to manipulate his *dream* and *thought* environments. Seth said man has Inner Senses, and when we consciously learn to use them, we become co-creators of our reality. Our real environment is composed of our thoughts and emotions, and it is the *intensity* of a feeling, or thought, or mental image that is the important factor in determining its subsequent physical manifestation. The more intense the seed, the sooner the plant will materialize. Furthermore, the seeds that die here are born and thrive in other dimensions of reality!

These were some thoroughly mind-boggling concepts. Though they were nothing I had ever fathomed, Seth came through and calmly explained it all, in depth. Totally fascinated, I was also frightened by these revelations. I was not yet ready to take responsibility for my life, if such responsibility were possible. I shelved the book and went on to other metaphysical authors with new ideas and ways of thinking about the nature of life. None of them, however, helped me with Tim.

The Omega and the Alpha

"Quite literally you see what you want to see; and you see your own thoughts and emotional attitudes materialized in physical form. If changes are to occur, they must be mental and psychic changes. These will be reflected in your environment. Negative, distrustful, fearful, or degrading attitudes toward anyone work against the self."

Seth, The Seth Material, *Chap. 13*

We lived in a former cinderblock garage economically converted by the hard-working Mexican-American owners into a one-bedroom rental apartment. Located in a sleepy village, a green oasis in the Southwest desert, this unique dwelling consisted of two main rooms (a combined kitchen/living room and a bedroom) in addition to one closet and one tiny bathroom. A one-inch gap between the bottom of the double doors and the frame that accessed the living room from outdoors allowed giant cockroaches to enter and leave at their whim.

Being "flower children," we weren't concerned about such trivial details. Tim would routinely knock his shoes out each morning before putting them on to remove any hidden critters. I would stuff towels under the bedroom door to have some semblance of peace while we slept. It never occurred to us to try to fix the gap. Rent was cheap. We did paint the rooms a bright yellow and orange, and I sewed flowered curtains to replace the former dingy ones.

The first couple of years of our marriage, we lived a fairly normal life. Work kept us occupied as we tried to adjust to our quite opposite personalities. We were continually surprising, and irritating, each other with our differing attitudes of what constituted a pleasant life. Tim taught grade school for a year and a half, but in order to retain his position, he needed to complete some college courses. He tried during the summer months, but his heart was never in it. Since I was working, he would undertake odd jobs occasionally while his main energy went to his music.

At first, I didn't mind. In the early years, I would often join the boys at nightly practice and gigs and have a good time. But as the years passed, our relationship never solidified into a compatible unit.

The marriage was, by all accounts, a total disaster. Hal had been right. In lieu of starting a family as we had planned after our fifth wedding anniversary, Tim decided to go on the road with his band. With my sincere blessings. Our agreement conveniently ignored, I finally had to admit I could not live with this man. Our interests and desires in life were totally dissimilar. Nor was I the kind of person to try to change someone. People were what they were, and what Tim was, was not what I wanted for a husband.

One day, driving to the second job I had to pay bills my husband refused to be concerned about or help with, I knew the marriage was over. It was just a matter of time for all of the details to be resolved. I was in the deepest slump ever. Never one to give up easily, I knew I could no longer continue this charade of a marriage. It devastated me that my marriage had failed. But now, I was late for work due to problems at the bank, and would not have time to go home and change clothes. I would be standing on three-inch heels for eight more hours. Thoroughly stressed, I drove on as I contemplated my situation. My soul ached; I was depressed, disillusioned, and heartsick.

In this state, knowing the decision to end my marriage had been made, I began thinking, for probably the first time in my life, "What did I want? If I could really, truly have it, what would I want?" Seriously considering the idea, I emphatically thought, "I want someone to love me. I want a kind, good man. One who will cherish and care for me as much as I do him. One who would love me, really love me, just the way I am." Fame, fortune, or money didn't interest me. With love, I could do anything.

Never before had I experienced such clarity of thought. Never before had I been more focused. For five brief minutes, desire for such a being consumed me and electrified my soul. My imagination blossomed at the thought of what a life would be like where I was totally and completely loved.

After returning to my former state of dejection, I wondered if there really *was* such a thing as a decent, kind man in this world. Did any actually exist? Having little faith in my abilities, in my intense anguish I thought, "If there is *any* Source of Goodness, *any* Source of Power that cares about me, help me now. I would do anything to meet such a man. I don't care what he looks like or how old he is, just as long as he accepts me and really loves *me*."

When I realized what I was doing, I stopped, disgusted with myself. It didn't work that way. There was no Power that was going to intrude on my life and suddenly make it right. It never had before, and it wouldn't now. I was the only one who could change my life.

I walked into the crowded bistro and sighed to myself, "Damn, it's busy tonight."

The other waitress gave me a sour look as I approached her. "Well, it's about time you got here," she grumbled. She had had to work an hour longer because I was late.

I was in no mood to bicker. "It wasn't my fault," I said, "I got here as soon as I could."

Still bitter and slightly drunk, she said, "Oh, sure, it wasn't your fault. Whose fault was it then?"

After defending myself to no avail, I decided to ignore her, and began cleaning tables. "God, what was I doing here?" I thought, "I don't need this abuse … Gees, I don't even drink!" The litany, "Bills, Bills, Bills," went through my mind. "Your wonderful husband thought this would be the ideal place for you to bring in some extra money while he drove off and played in the wild blue yonder, you fool," one part of my mind commented. I sighed, "God, when would I ever quit listening to that idiot?" and, in the next inner breath, answered myself, "Soon, darn soon."

Little more than an hour later, the door to the establishment opened and the man of my dreams walked into my life. I was immediately drawn to him. He was handsome, appeared to be a little older than I, but somehow, in the pit of my stomach, I recognized him. We were introduced by mutual friends that night, and hit it off from the start.

Bob was kind, intelligent, charming, creative, and a perfect gentleman. He was everything I imagined I would want in a man, except that he was quite a bit older than me. The instant compatibility and

25

rightness of the relationship could not be denied, however. Two years after my divorce from Tim went through, after much soul-searching because of the twenty-two year age difference, we followed our hearts and were married.

Discovery

"In a very real manner, events or objects are actually focal points where highly charged psychic impulses are transformed into something that can be physically perceived: a breakthrough into matter. When such highly charged impulses intersect or coincide, matter is formed. The reality behind such an explosion into matter is independent of the matter itself. An identical or nearly identical pattern may reemerge 'at any time' again and again, if the proper coordinates exist for activation."

Seth, The Seth Material, *Chap. 10*

B ob's first wife, Del, had died of cancer in 1971, the year I married Tim. Bob had remained single after her demise until we married in 1979. Del was a full-blooded American Dakota Sioux Indian. Born on a reservation in upstate New York, her adult life had revolved around her Indian heritage. A dedicated advocate of the Indian plight, she had lobbied most of her life to lessen injustices toward the Indian People.

One day, not long after we were married, Bob and I were organizing our combined households. One folder was filled with some of Del's Indian records. In the folder, among copies of letters to various Congressmen, were some old photographs of Indians she had collected over the years. A chill ran down my spine as I picked up one of the pictures. *There was my Indian brave*! There he was, no mistake about it, the same hair, face, stance.

"Bob, do you know who this is?" I asked, trying to remain calm.

Bob glanced at the photograph. "No, those are just some old pictures Del had when I married her."

I looked closer at the picture. Not only was this my Indian brave, but I was now certain it was *this picture* I had seen! How on earth could that be possible? There had been some incongruities to the previous event I had never been able to figure out. The Indian had looked real enough beside my bedside those many years ago, in fact, exactly as he did in this photograph. But he had had no flesh tones. And this was a black- and-white photograph!

I sat back as memories rushed into my mind. There had also been a background behind the Indian. Not the bedroom itself, but one of desert rock and shrubs. The same background I now saw in this blasted photograph! Damn.

I looked at the picture, still not believing that I held it in my hands. A doubtful memory surfaced. Didn't I think he had been holding a tomahawk? There was none in the photograph, but his right arm was bent and raised to shoulder height, with his hand almost over his head. Well, he didn't have one, but to a very frightened person, I could see where it might look as if he did.

I couldn't believe it. I turned the picture over; there was no date on the photograph, but the name White Plume was written in pencil. I shook my head in amazement. "Bob, you're never going to believe this, but I would swear this is the same Indian brave I saw standing beside my bed years ago when I had just married Tim."

"Are you sure?" he asked, dubiously.

"Positive," I said, emphatically. "Seeing this picture brings the entire scene back to me." After several more minutes of reflection, I shook my head and said, "I'd stake my life on the fact that it was he. Don't you remember anything about this picture?"

Bob looked at the photograph again. "No, I don't remember Del ever mentioning him. Maybe it was someone she knew before I met her. That's possible, but I don't recognize him or his name."

I sat there, practically in shock, no longer interested in household chores. What possible explanation could there be for such phenomena? How could a photograph appear full-size and real enough to frighten me so many years ago? I wanted to tear it to shreds. I wanted the picture erased from existence as we knew it. Why was this happening to me? What had I ever done to deserve these mysteries in my life? I set the photograph down with a heavy sigh. This picture and its appearance, then and now, went against everything I had been taught to be true. Reality was not as simple as it seemed.

White Plume photograph discovered 8 years after the vision.

The Straw

Now it seems to you, of course, that you are the only consious part of yourself, for you are identifying with the actor in this particular production. The other portions of your multidimensional personality, in these other reincarnational plays, are also conscious, however. And because you <u>are</u> a multidimensional consciousness, 'you' are also conscious in other realities beside these.

Seth, Seth Speaks, *Session 521*

In the year 1980, I began an intense period of concentration as I entered college. For three years I did little but study for my bachelor's degree in Computer Science. When I had time for recreational reading, science fiction novels were my usual form of stimulating entertainment. My interest in metaphysics was not gone, however, just dormant.

It was Christmas, 1982, and we were visiting relatives in North Dakota over the holidays. Everyone was in a festive mood despite the cold winter night enveloping the farm house. The eight-foot-high tree was festooned in decorations; the lights beautifully illuminated the rich, timber-lined walls and ceiling. A wood fire in the white rock fireplace splashed the surroundings with shades of gold; the mantle was strewn with candles, evergreen and numerous stockings. Anxious young nieces and nephews tried to stay awake for the arrival of Santa Claus.

Good cheer was the prevalent atmosphere as we began to fill all the available bed and floor space of the big house. Laughter from the rest of the family filtered into our room as we prepared for bed. The blankets felt good as we snuggled into them. A smile lingered on my face as the events of the day passed through my mind. Eventually, total relaxation gradually removed the smile and dispersed the thoughts.

The bedroom became another place. Gone was the wood paneling. Gone were the wall hangings. Gone was the warm embrace of the rural household. I was now outdoors.

Blue sky graced the horizon. I was lying low, presumably on the ground, when I looked up. A sixty-year-old American Indian was hurrying toward me. A look of concern furrowed his brow. Dressed in buckskins and a full headdress, feathers flowing down his back, he bent over my prone body, looked me straight in the eyes, then searched my face with solicitude. Surprised, I immediately realized I wasn't where I was supposed to be, nor was I in the company of the person I was supposed to be. I became alarmed and jerked upright.

The room returned to its correct physical state with my abrupt movement, and I disturbed Bob. After I explained to him what had happened, we lay back down, and Bob was soon fast asleep. A seething cauldron of thoughts kept me from joining him.

This had been no illusory dream. It was as real and immediate as it could possibly be. There was no gradual phasing in and out. There were no hallucinatory dream images. I was here one minute and there the next, through absolutely no effort on my part! I lay on my back, restless, eyes wide open. Fear, doubt, anger, panic, and confusion vied for dominance of my emotions. Finally calming down, my innate curiosity caused some coherent thoughts to surface.

Genuinely perplexed, I thought of all my experiences. All had taken place when I was happy. All had taken place in, or were related to, the Old West... Swinging between logic and emotion, I thought irritably, I didn't even like Westerns. I rarely read them or saw movies about them. I had no interest in nor reason to be interested in Frontier existence, I thought emphatically. No reason ... when it occurred to me... or did I? Could my experiences have anything to do with Del's book?

A Good Day to Die was published by Doubleday and described the life of Del's great-grandfather, Gray Wolf, a Dakota Sioux warrior. It was an excellent book, extremely well written, about a remarkable man. One of the few Westerns I had ever read. But what could the connection be? He had lived for some time in both Apache and Dakota territory. This included both New Mexico and North Dakota ... and I stopped as the thought hit me ... *Two places where I had resided and where I had experienced all of my "visions."*

33

As this revelation sunk in, I thought of my "visions." The first two occurred long before I met Bob or had been aware of the book, so there couldn't have been unconscious bleedthroughs due to familiarity with the material. Was there some kind of reincarnational relationship connecting Del's great-grandfather and me? Was that what the "visions" were telling me? Was this some kind of incarnational awareness I was experiencing? Then, what of the White Plume photograph? The Chief had looked nothing like him, that I could tell, and this "episode" was in full, brilliant color and motion!

Unable to pace to release my frustrated energy, I clenched my teeth in aggravation. Well, enough, I thought. I may not understand, but this third encounter settled it. I *was* going to find out all I could on metaphysics. Though not totally ignorant of the subject, I was not well-versed in it either. Without informing anyone else what had happened, upon returning home I ordered more metaphysical literature.

Paradox

If you could understand to begin with that <u>you</u> are a spirit, and therefore free of space and time yourself, then you could at least consider the possibility that some such messages were coming to you from other portions of your own reality.

Seth, The Unknown Reality, *Vol. 1, Session 684*

O ne peaceful morning at 3:00 a.m., I responded to the cries of our six-month-old son. In May 1984 I graduated from college, and within three months while working on my Master's degree, discovered I was pregnant. Bob and I, in due time, were blessed with a beautiful 8-pound, 4-ounce baby boy who brought more joy to us than we thought possible.

After changing his wet diaper, I sat in the rocking chair nursing him. The lights were low to encourage my precious bundle to return to sleep. I was groggy and hoping to return to bed myself in a few minutes. Suddenly, I was wide awake and disturbed. Someone was in the room with us.

I remained calm so as not to alarm the baby, but I almost stopped breathing in my astonishment. All of my senses alert, I slowly turned my eyes to where I felt the "intruder." I could *see* nothing, but I knew someone was in the room with us. I could *feel* him, or her, standing about four feet in front of us. I returned my gaze to my son's face and froze in position. Brian was my primary concern. I didn't want anything to happen to him, or for him to be upset by anything.

I was about to accept that I was imagining things when the baby soon convinced me that I was not. Without any prompting or untoward movement by me, Brian suddenly stopped sucking, let go of the nipple, and turned his head 180 degrees in the direction of the visitor. My eyes were still concentrated on his face, and I saw his sweet brown eyes actually light up in delight and a big smile come over his face.

I was astounded! My God, Brian could feel it and obviously see it, too! I didn't know what to think or do. I sat there, frightened, wondering what to do, with my eyes still glued to my son's face. Then a curious thing happened. I heard, in my mind, the figure admonish Brian! It told him to go back to his nursing, as he was scaring his mother. The figure said he, or she, would meet with Brian later.

Shocked at what I was hearing, I was even more alarmed when Brian immediately responded. He got an astonished look on his face, glanced up at me as if to verify what the figure had just told him, and turned back to his meal after a final chagrined glance at our invisible guest.

I was beside myself. What was going on?! Who was messing with me and my baby?! I was not happy and no longer sleepy. Brian had obviously handled the situation better than I had. I felt no malevolent forces; in fact, there seemed to be a lightness emanating from the area; but after the figure chastised my son, I finally had the presence of mind to mentally ask the visitor to leave. I then used a metaphysical technique of imagining a protective force field around our home. Though I didn't believe in evil entities, I was taking no chances where my son was concerned. The presence vanished, and I was left in my bewilderment. The baby finished nursing and dropped off to sleep in my arms.

After returning Brian to his crib, I was faced once again with my apparent ignorance of what I had just experienced. I had no idea who or what had graced us with its presence. The fact that Brian became aware of and responded with pleasure to the "guest" while engaged in the most important aspect of life at that age, eating and being nurtured by his mother, put me in somewhat of a quandary. After returning to bed myself, I tossed and turned the rest of the night trying to figure out who had visited us.

Memories

The one self that he [man] recognizes is the only part of himself of which he is presently aware. Other facts of consciousness available to him, and a part of his greater nature, appear foreign, or "not-self," or "beyond self," because of the focus of selectivity as it now operates.

Seth, The Unknown Reality, *Vol. 1, Session 684*

The next day I told Bob of the ordeal. He was unconcerned and fascinated. "You know, Del had something similar happen to her when she was young. She was about five or six years old and had just moved to Nicaragua to live with her Aunt and Uncle. She was lying in bed and, evidently, it got real cold. She was too young and frightened to ask for anything, so she just remained there shivering. She said her dead mother came to her and covered her with a blanket. The next day, her relatives were astonished that she had the blanket. She was too short to have reached the high shelf where the blanket was kept. They checked with everyone in the house, and no one had given her the blanket." He paused, then said, "And, of course, you remember Dad's experiences."

Yes, I remembered. All of them. Yet the one that

stood out in my mind now was the one he had spoken of at Thanksgiving dinner, 1977, when Bob and I were first dating. One I would never forget.

Bob, his parents, and I were celebrating the holiday together. Over the preferred steak dinner, the conversation had somehow shifted to metaphysical affairs.

"I have never told anyone this before," Ben began. "The most wonderful thing happened at our wedding... there was a brilliant White Light present at the ceremony."

"Really!" I said, enthusiastically.

"Yes, we both saw it, and so did others at the ceremony."

"How wonderful!" I commented, giving both of them an admiring smile, "That must have made you feel great! Starting out like that."

Ben hesitated at my interruption. Realizing he had more to say on the subject, I restrained myself, and he continued. "After the services when I was waiting in the back seat of the car for Edna to come out, a Being of Light appeared across from me. He told me that this marriage would bear great fruit. That great good would result from this union."

"Wow!" I said, totally impressed. Irrepressibly enthusiastic, since I did find psychic phenomena interesting, I asked, "Who do you think it was?"

Sudden silence filled the dining room. As I took another forkful of food, Ben's wife looked down at her plate, obviously upset by my question. Ben finished chewing what was in his mouth and said, "It was

God. Jesus Christ blessed our marriage himself."

I almost choked on my food, but controlled myself. I glanced at Bob—who was no Christian; he was, in fact, more inclined toward metaphysical beliefs than Christianity—as he studiously inspected his plate. I said something conciliatory, but mentally I sighed. When would I ever learn to keep my mouth shut? But I couldn't help my honest reactions. Why did people think every Spirit visitation was a visit from a God? I respected both of his parents and knew, without a doubt, that the event actually occurred. Their interpretation of the event, who it had been, was what I questioned.

As the memory ended, I thought of all these related experiences. There had to be something more to them. All of us had seen, or felt, something. Did Del see her mother because she believed in ancestral survival after death, and that her mother would come to her aid when she needed her? Did Ben see Jesus Christ because those were his beliefs? Did I see no form, but felt one, because I had no preconceived idea what life would look like after death? Did Brian see what was really there because he had not yet been trained to believe such events were impossible? Was the energy the same in all the cases and merely "formed" according to our divergent belief systems?

I shook my head. I wasn't very pleased that a spirit, or something, would come to my home. I preferred that spirits would stay where they belonged. It seemed I had more reading to do.

Dream Life

In this state [the deep dream state] you also pursue works or endeavors that may or may not be connected with your interests as you know them. You are learning, studying, playing; you are anything but asleep (smile) as you think of the term.

Seth, Seth Speaks, *Session 531*

A bride emerged from a modern airplane. Standing at the top of the exit ramp, I was the bride dressed in a stunning, full-length black wedding gown. The dress was quite beautiful, and I remember being awed by its splendor but disturbed by its color. I hoped that it didn't portend trouble, but somehow, I had been reassured and subjectively knew that the outcome of events would be beneficial.

This was one of the few dreams I could remember from my youth. After my first unfortunate marriage and my second wonderful one, I knew the dream had symbolically foreseen my circumstances at least ten years before they had occurred.

My personal investigation of the "strange occurrences" in my life began with the only "spiritual" part of myself I could confidently contact on a regular basis - my dreams. I had read that dreams were meaningful, an important counterpart to physical reality, and that much could be learned *about* reality by becoming familiar with that aspect of being. Just prior to sleep, I began telling myself I would remember my dreams and write them down when I awoke.

Since I had paid so little attention to my dreams in the past, I was somewhat intrigued by what I now found. Among the usual fare that dealt with everyday problems and situations, there were some that stood out for their "other worldly" qualities.

Some impressed me for their absolute beauty. I visited towering mountain areas of intense, scintillating clarity. Sun glinted off snow-covered forests; lush, verdant valleys spread below me. Crystal-clear, tree-lined lakes enchanted me, as did charming ocean vistas. All were in vibrant, achingly magnificent color. Energy emanated from these dreams, and I awoke from them feeling physically revitalized and refreshed.

Other dreams puzzled me in that I was being introduced to significant strangers. In those dreams I attended several parties and met intriguingly charismatic, highly intelligent people. Unaccountably drawn to them, I awoke wondering why they affected me so. I recognized none of the participants, and none of the events reflected any physical circumstances or desires on my part.

A whole world of activity was going on while I slept. I was attending classes and being taught in my dreams. Once I was learning things about memory and the proper way to remember. Another time I was given instruction in the metaphysical techniques necessary to divine the future and find meaning in events. Each time I would awaken with vague details of what had actually transpired, but frequently I was being tested, and most often, I passed my dream exams. In the spring of 1986, quite out of season, I had four dreams in which I was receiving Christmas presents.

The Gift

Illness and suffering are not thrust upon you by God, or by All That Is, or by an outside agency. They are a by-product of the learning process, created by you, in themselves quite neutral. On the other hand, your existence itself, the reality and nature of your planet, the whole existence in which you have these experiences, are also created by you, using the abilities of which I have spoken.

Seth, Seth Speaks, *Session 580*

I sat across from my doctor. I really did like my gynecologist. Now, however, I was somewhat tense being in her office. I had had a routine pap smear several weeks ago, and the nurse called yesterday to say the doctor wanted to see me.

"Your pap smear came back positive," the doctor said, somewhat nervously. "The results show you have severe dysplasia." Noting my blank facial expression, she continued, "This means the cells change and move when they shouldn't."

"What does that mean? Why would my cells ..."

"There is a possibility of melanoma."

"I have cancer?!" I practically shouted. Good God! Cancer! My mind went numb. I half heard the doctor reassure me that it was a slow-growing type of cancer and to begin making plans for a definitive biopsy. I rose, mouthing platitudes that I was fine in response to the doctor's soft-spoken queries, and wandered out the door.

Feeling as though my breath had been knocked out of me, I tried to comprehend what I had just been told. Gees, I could die. I had a year-old baby; I couldn't die. He needed me. I had a wonderful husband. One who would be devastated if a second wife of his died of cancer. The first death had been quite painful for him, another would kill him. How was I ever going to tell him? I tried to get a grip on myself. I had others to think of besides myself.

After getting off my shaky legs, I sat in the car waiting for the air conditioner to cool off the constant desert heat. Why was this happening to me? I didn't feel sick. I wasn't in severe pain, only in occasional pain, which I had attributed to normal female life. I guess it was more than that, I thought with a sigh.

But why? Why was I sick? Emotionally this was the happiest time of my life. I had people who loved me and whom I loved around me. I had a good education which would always enable me to support myself. If mind created matter, as sages said, why did I have cervical cancer? Thoughts of Tim and his infidelity, thoughts of minor sexual abuse as a child, even thoughts of my dear Bob's reluctance to have children all entered my head. Since I did believe we create our reality through our beliefs, intent, and pattern of thought, I obviously needed to look at my belief structure. What I was creating was not good.

Before I drove into the heavy afternoon traffic, I tried to comprehend the reason for the cancer manifestation. What thoughts, what beliefs did I harbor that were making me sick? Cancer of the sex organs. That was specific enough. I obviously held some conflict regarding sexual relations. Thoughts of old boyfriends entered my mind. Then it dawned on me. Of course. I had a belief, a hidden one to be sure, that all men wanted from me was sex.

My body was rebelling. It knew this belief to be untrue, but until "I" accepted this belief to be untrue, my cells would react to my beliefs and make me ill. My body was confused by the unconscious belief I was sending it - there was something wrong with sex. But its innate knowledge knew that there was nothing wrong with sex. It was a highly natural, enjoyable, wonderful aspect of life.

I took a moment to forgive myself for causing this disease to appear in my life. I wondered what "hidden" beliefs I held that could further adversely affect my life. Well, I would soon find out. This would not continue. From this point on, every emotion I encountered was questioned to determine the reason, or belief, behind its manifestation. Each erroneous belief, as I perceived it, was evaluated and replaced with a more positive one as needed. I would have a lovely life.

Awakening

The inner self, as distinguished from the more accessible subconscious, is aware of the situation [illness] and finds release through frequent inner communications where successes are remembered and reexperienced. The dream state becomes an extremely vivid time, for such experiences assure the personality of its larger nature. It knows it is more than the self that it has for a time chosen to be.

Seth, The Seth Material, *Chap. 11*

An eighty-year-old woman was getting married, for the first time, to a man who had been married twelve times before! The woman was nervous and kept asking a friend named Lydia for reassurance.

The minister came out wearing one of those tall hats of Jewish, or Greek Orthodox, tradition. He smiled and said that since we had a few minutes before the ceremony, he had some food for us to eat. He began passing around baklava, an ethnic pastry. We all partook as the minister proceeded to hand out two books. One was called *Hester Street*, and the other *Little Women*. *Hester Street* was about prostitutes or dancers, and *Little Women* showed the contrast between women, especially the virtuous ones.

As the minister gave us the books, I noticed a Christmas tree made out of white candles placed in tiers. It was quite alluring, with the flames flickering hypnotically. As I was admiring this sight, I was presented with a greeting card. The card was white and uniquely designed in that it opened in the center of the page, hinged on the left and right edges. Each half of the page was diagonally cut into a side view silhouette of a face. When flat, the two faces met, as if kissing. Above these carved figures, on the front of the card was the printing:

> Of All the Occult Sciences
> and of All the Spells

When I opened the window of the faces, on the inside page was the printing:

> Just Remember, I'm the One
> that Bewitched You First.

I awoke and quickly wrote down the dream. "Wow, what was that?!" I thought, totally awed. I had never had such a vivid, more powerful dream in my life! My body actually tingled from the impact. I lay back and let the energy rush through me. "And poetry!" I thought, thoroughly delighted, "How adorable!" I quickly looked at my notes. What did it all mean?

I had never heard of the book *Hester Street*, but I was, of course, familiar with *Little Women*. I didn't know any older woman who was getting married, nor any Jews or prostitutes, or dancers, for that matter. Nor did I know anyone named Lydia - pretty name though. But the detail! The clarity and vividness of the dream! I could still see the card. It had been like holding one physically and reading it!

I smiled, got up, and started the day in a good mood. I supposed the dream could be symbolic of aspects of myself. All men and women to one extent or another have attributes of both promiscuity and virginity. But why an 80-year-old woman? Main characters in dreams often represent the dreamer herself. Could it mean that at age eighty I would experience some kind of union? Maybe the ultimate union? Was the dream telling me I wouldn't die for a long time yet? That was a reassuring thought, given the fact that I had been diagnosed as having cervical cancer last week. I brushed aside my concerns about that as I analyzed the dream.

Why poetry, though? Was this illustrating creative abilities lying hidden within myself? Or did the message contain its own significance? Occult sciences meant sciences dealing with the knowledge of supernatural or hidden influences on man's life. That was exactly what I was trying to learn! I knew nothing of spells nor did I believe it possible to influence someone unnaturally. The only one who could enchant me, I knew, was my Source or Higher Self.

I looked at the dream again. Symbolically, there was an imminent union, then nourishment or energy distributed. Knowledge in the form of books was acquired, and sacredness and beauty could be what the Christmas tree represented. The greeting card could have been just that, a greeting or introduction. I shook my head. Well, whatever it meant, it could happen again, anytime. It felt wonderful. Maybe my Source was just trying to cheer me up after my biopsy. And cheering up I could surely use. Bob was thoroughly upset but trying to hide it. I was concerned since both I and my son were still very young. But the doctor said minor surgery was supposed to take care of it...

Four days later, I quickly wrote down another dream upon awakening. Again, it had been an extremely clear one, of a scorpion on the wall near the ceiling of the hall window of our home. In the dream, I even had the presence of mind to ask how many scorpions had been in the house up to this time. I was given the answer eight.

I laid down my pen and thought little of the dream. We hadn't had any scorpions in the house in quite a while. Weeks ago Bob had checked and reinforced all of the seals around the doors where we suspected the critters came in. Maybe I had repressed fears about them.

I quickly dressed and left the bedroom. As I turned the corner I couldn't help but see the hall window, and I stopped in my tracks. Near the top of the window was a huge scorpion, right where my dream had said it would be!

I called Bob over and he disposed of it. It was a ten-foot-high window, and while up there, he found a hole which hadn't been properly sealed when the house was built where the scorpion had obviously entered the house. We were both delighted with the dream help. The precognitive gift from the spirit world reinforced my hope that my efforts were bearing good fruit.

Soul Sight

Consciousness is an attribute of the soul, a tool that can be turned in many directions. You are not your consciousness. It is something that belongs to you and to the soul. You are learning to use it. To the extent that you understand and utilize the various aspects of consciousness, you will learn to understand your own reality, and the conscious self will truly become conscious.

Seth, Seth Speaks, *Session 575*

A sigh of contentment passed my lips as I lay down on the waterbed. I had recently received another bill of clear health from my gynecologist. No evidence of cancer showed itself after having undergone minor surgery two years ago. Life was good.

During the past year, I had begun routinely relaxing when Brian took his daily nap. Chasing after a robust child took a lot of energy from my thirty-six-year old body, and I had learned to rest when he did. I rarely slept but would balance between consciousness and sleep, relaxed but alert for any sound from my three-year-old son. This floating, alpha state always refreshed me and gave me the energy to crawl on the floor and play trucks for several more hours before Bob came home from work.

Lying there, totally relaxed, I became aware of a book materialized before my closed eyes! It was right in front of my face, distinct as could be. I seemed to be reading it, or another part of myself was reading it, until I noticed the book and it immediately disappeared.

I sat up in consternation. There was that book again. This was about the third time I had "caught" myself reading it! I picked up my notebook from the bedside table and wrote down what I had seen. It was a normal book. Lines of text of distinct, printed material, and part of "myself" was reading it. I couldn't remember any of what I had read, but it had all made perfect sense while "I" was reading it.

I set down the notebook, deep in thought. Inner Sight. It must be Inner Sight. Wow. It actually existed. And I was using it! Soul Sight. The ability to contact and interact with the spirit part of life. The part of life from which we came and into which we would return upon physical death. We accessed it constantly in our dreams, of course, but it could, so they said, also be consciously accessed before death.

From all of my past metaphysical studies I knew it was possible, but how was I doing it? Intrigued, I decided to try to catch myself in the act, so to speak, and analyze the mechanics involved. If I could reach this spiritual realm, I wanted to be able to control my visits. I knew it was a latent talent we all possessed, but which most of us ignored or didn't know existed. If I could develop this ability, I could find answers to life directly, I thought. No hearsay or fears or dogma need dictate my beliefs. I would know. My determination solidified, a plan of action took form.

The next day I lay down again, anxious to see what would happen. While lying there I watched the thoughts drift through my mind. Nothing happened. The next day, I tried again and nothing happened. The next day and the next, nothing happened. Tense as a tightened screw, I lay there waiting for it to happen again. Nothing would.

Undaunted, I tried different recommended techniques known to facilitate contact with the spiritual plane. I tried progressively relaxing my body. After days of this, I discovered that didn't work; while my body was relaxed, my mind just raced. I tried blanking out my thoughts with no success. Imagining my body as being very heavy and "me" being very light didn't bring results either. I concentrated on the third eye area, (the middle of the forehead, between the brows) for days, and just gave myself headaches. No Soul Sight. No matter what I did, nothing else would happen. After six weeks of effort, I became totally aggravated and admitted my inability to duplicate contact. I quit watching my mind, or doing anything but relax, and *had another vision.*

This one was of Bob, three-dimensionally, quite vividly standing beside our bed as if he were waiting for me to join him. Physically, he was asleep beside me. I noticed this sight consciously, then rolled over and fell asleep myself. Bob had no recollection of the event. Every day after this I would lie down, wait for the Soul Sight to be activated, and I gradually discovered the clues I needed. I learned I must just float, remove all thoughts of my body, ignore it entirely, let it relax and just drift in the alpha state, and my Soul Sight would engage.

In October 1988, I had four "visions"; in November, one; and in December, five. The situation was frustrating at first. As soon as my conscious mind became aware of a spiritual scene, it would immediately close off the experience. The first five were rather ordinary views of Bob or Brian, or of printed material I was trying to read. The books, when they entered my awareness, were particularly challenging. Whenever I tried to focus on the words, they would change into different words, or letters, and I could not quite grasp what was written. It all made perfect sense *before* I tried to concentrate on the pages, but the comprehension and memory of the text always left me.

There was nothing ordinary about the sightings themselves, however! It was as if an aperture opened on my forehead in between my eyebrows, and a complete three-dimensional scene replaced the featureless background seen when the eyes are closed. It was not dreamlike, but was vivid, clear, and immediate. It was a conscious awareness of, and sometimes, involvement in, an activity.

Flight

You are focused in a daily life for a reason. You have adopted it as a challenge. But within its framework you are also meant to grow and develop, and to <u>extend</u> the limits of your consciousness. It is very difficult to admit that you are in many ways more effective and creative in the sleep state than in the waking state, and somewhat shattering to admit the dream body can indeed fly, defying both time and space. It is much easier to pretend that all experiences are symbolic and not literal, to evolve complicated psychological theories, for example, to explain flying dreams.

Seth, Seth Speaks, *Session 538*

A beautiful meadow filled with red and gold flowers spread before me. Poppies came to mind, and a girl in brown peasant garb was walking in the midst of them.

The scene vanished, and I was back in my physical bed. Left with only a memory, I relaxed again and soon "saw," using Soul Sight, a woman I recognized. The woman was someone Bob and I had once met at South Padre Island in Texas. White-haired, tanned and wrinkled, the woman looked surprisingly like a picture we had taken of her while she gave a lecture outdoors. While lying there, I recalled our visit with her and remembered seeing a seagull fly by, thinking it might be fun to be one. The next thing I knew...

I was soaring over the water like a bird. I could see the water below me and actually feel the wind current lift my body. It was simply heavenly! The air actually supported me like an ocean wave would support a bubble. Riding the air waves. Gliding over the unseen currents. The ease of flight was delightful! I luxuriated in this sensation for a while when I became curious as to how I was doing this. I looked over at my outspread left arm, and it was no longer an arm. It was a bird's wing!! The white feathers were suddenly being bent by a contrary wind.

The shock of the sight, and the fear of what the bent feathers might portend, brought me right back to physical reality.

I fairly leaped from my bed in my excitement. Good God, what a treat! I had heard of out-of-body experiences where one was out of the physical body, fully conscious and aware of being in a spiritual environment; and I imagined that this was my first such experience, but I had not yet read of many transformations such as mine. But I couldn't deny what I had sensed. I felt the wind, and I felt what seemed like my feathers being ruffled. Good Lord, life was strange! I was ecstatic for days.

It was several months before I experienced anything remotely similar to this event, but the Soul Sight continued, and each "vision" held a valuable lesson for me. A new awareness.

I "saw" an unfamiliar room, viewed from an odd angle, with antique furniture in it. I "saw" my hands, but in a different position than my physical hands. I "saw" the bedroom I was in and the furniture in it. I "saw" dancers, ballet dancers I thought, in brightly colored gauzy skirts. I "saw" other rooms in my house than the one I was in physically, and frequently I "saw" Brian when he was actually asleep in his own bedroom. I "saw" minute, colorful, sparkling particles in the air around me.

Though each incident was an adventure come to life, I tried to detect a logical pattern that might define or unite the events. No such pattern revealed itself to my scrutiny. I was aware I was experiencing enticingly real Soul Sight, but that was all I could definitely say at the time.

A Voice in the Night

The body's innate knowledge, then, will try to
translate itself often into psychological activity that
may result in hunches, premonitions, and so forth.
The senses may be utilized to clarify the message.
You might hear a voice mentally, for example, or see a
flashing image.

Seth, The Unknown Reality, *Vol. 1*

On March 8, 1989 I went up to bed in a happy, contented mood. I decided, since I felt so good, to try for an out-of-body experience (OOBE). For weeks, whenever I remembered to do it, just before sleep I would imagine, visualize, myself standing in the hallway outside our bedroom on the second floor of the house. This night, I honestly can't remember if I did or not. I know I did progressively tense then relax all of the muscles in my body. I took a few deep breaths.

When my body became quite rigid, I ignored it, turned my eyes upward and concentrated on the middle of my forehead. As I did so, thoughts of a dying relative crossed my mind. He had been sick for some time, and I wondered when he would pass on. The next thing I knew ...

I was walking down the stairs in the hall outside our bedroom to the entranceway near our front door. When I reached the tile flooring of the first floor, I stopped in surprise. The door leading outdoors was open about a foot. Perplexed, I wondered why the door was open. It should be closed. I looked around the foyer. Nothing seemed amiss. Then a thought struck me. Was there an intruder in the house? Fear streaked through my body. With that thought and a lightening fast recoiling sensation, I was immediately back in my physical body.

I had been out of body. I had succeeded. But was the door really open? I listened intently for several minutes. There didn't appear to be any noises coming from the lower level of the house. Should I get up and check the door? I debated whether to do that, or to wake up Bob. I rejected both possibilities. I knew the door was closed. It must have been some aberration or hallucinatory aspect of the spiritual environment. After listening for a few more minutes, I finally relaxed and snuggled back into the waterbed.

Without warning, a distinct male voice spoke from my left, from the vicinity of my nightstand. "The end is near," he said, ominously.

I jerked back in astonishment, and said in my mind, "What?!!"

Whereupon the voice calmly repeated the message. Shocked, I sat upright, looked around the partially lighted room, my heart pounding. No one was in the room with us. Reassured but shaken, I lay back down. Then fright set in, and in somewhat of a panic I began questioning, "What end?! My end?! The world's end?!!" Totally confused and scared, I lay there trying to figure out what the message meant. Exhaustion eventually overcame me and I fell asleep.

The next morning, still ignorant over the meaning of the midnight message, I received a telephone call from my mother. She informed me that my Uncle had died at 9:00 that morning, and I learned the "truth" of the nocturnal communication. The end was near. That was what the voice meant. Just before my out-of-body experience, I had been thinking of my sick Uncle. I had received an answer to my question.

Dimensions

*In physical life there is a lag between the conception
of an idea and its physical construction. In dream
reality, this is not so.*

Seth, Seth Speaks, *Session 538*

The spiritual dimension defied definition.
Though I was totally, completely intrigued
by it all, mesmerized by the awesome
wonder of true reality, never was I able to anticipate
or predict what would occur there or when I would
reach that dimension. The "visions" did continue on
a more or less regular basis, but not frequently
considering I relaxed daily in anticipation. The
content of each visit varied, but each rest period
quite often held various scenes. When my ego
became aware of a scene, it would immediately cut
off or censor the view. I would again relax, and
another excursion would ensue.

3-8-89

I was aware that I was out-of-body and going
through a floor interior. There were fibers and dirt
hanging from the joints of the flat building-material
surfaces.

3-18-89

Distinct masses of clouds edged in vibrant,
golden sunlight colors.

4-10-89

A young blonde boy, maybe ten years old, reaching down directly toward my face as if he were scooping up something from the ground (a ball?).

4-11-89

A marble or stone pillar wrapped round with a rope and anchor attached to it.

The ceiling above me; a television set which was turned on; and the side of our refrigerator downstairs, with the notes attached to it by heart-shaped and picture magnets. (Could I have drifted into the townhouse beyond our common wall and seen the neighbors' TV?)

4-18-89

I was hovering over a street near the apartments where I once lived in town. A bright yellow and orange minivan with a sharp-edged hood, unlike any I have ever seen in this reality, pulled into the street. There was someone sitting in the front passenger seat, but I couldn't get a good look at her. My viewpoint was from above the cars. (Was this a probable me? Another me who was experiencing some of the choices I didn't choose to experience in this reality?)

Saw Brian, and was reading a book again. The inside cover of the book had swirling designs on it like in old books. I was reading sentences and turning pages, but couldn't quite grasp what I had read.

4-19-89

The back cushions of the beige and brown loveseat downstairs, and then, our bedroom. Reading, again.

4-24-89

The ocean, then a room with a bed, like in a

hotel. (The word apple popped into my mind after the scene dissolved. Might this refer to New York as the location of the scene?)

5-1-89

Brian, then upon returning (i.e., the Soul Sight was no longer activated), and exiting (the Soul Sight was active again), a newspaper column which looked like the obituaries with names listed and text underneath.

Later this evening, friends visited and informed us that they had just returned from an out-of-town funeral. We had known nothing of the death, the people involved, nor of their trip. This excursion appears to indicate precognition of our friends' news!

5-2-89

The head of a man with nostril holes in his mouth, above his teeth (i.e., no nose). The word abnormality came into my mind, and immediately a very vivid image of Bob.

This was strange. I wasn't frightened by the image. It was all quite matter of fact. Several hours later, Bob came home from work early. He had a sore throat and was really tired. This was sudden, as there was no indication that he was feeling ill when he left this morning. The sequence of images appears again to have been foresight, but this time, as an indication that Bob was feeling abnormal.

5-4-89

Brian's bedspread and corner of his room, as seen from the perspective of his doorway.

5-10-89

A breakthrough experience. I was in a playful mood as I lay down to relax today. After a few minutes of relaxation, I noticed my "inner" leg bend its knee and swing back and forth several times like a child's would while sitting on a bench. This wouldn't seem unusual considering the mood I was in, but *it was swinging through the physical bed I was lying on*! I could feel the spiritual leg push through the resilient layers of the covers, mattress, and frame of the waterbed. It was a strange, but not unpleasant, sensation. I was stunned back to physical awareness as soon as my conscious mind became aware of the "impossible" proceedings.

This was the first time I had sensed my spiritual body, the multi-dimensional counterpart to the physical body, functioning. I had seen parts of it before, my hands for instance, but this time I actually *felt* my spiritual legs. I knew I was progressing, however slowly, and was much encouraged by this event.

5-22-89

Two skeletal figures, their faces. Reminded me of the pictures of the Egyptian mummies we had taken at the Vatican Museum in Rome just after I graduated from college. The female seemed to move her head to look at the person next to her. The spectral face gave the appearance of being scared or dazed.

A little girl, about two or three years old, sitting in a railroad car passenger seat, or a 50's car seat. She had big eyes and was looking right at me, *as if she could see me*. She had short, dark, curly hair and wore old-fashioned clothes. She was moving around on the seat a little.

A tall, blonde man in a modern white suit. He seemed to be talking to me, or at least to someone, and moving toward me. I didn't recognize him.

Then, definite reading. Strongly felt it was material with which I am familiar. Next time I will get up and write it down, it was that clear.

5-30-89

A beautiful vista, looking down a modern street with well-tended houses on it. The sky was gorgeous, sunset colors. This was just after noon, physically.

5-31-89

A blonde woman with wavy, almost shoulder-length hair. She was in the grass, on one knee, talking to someone I couldn't see.

6-2-89

While relaxing I was thinking about aliens, if there really were such a thing.

Then, I saw a military man in a blue uniform and white hat walk next to a tall, circular structure. Was it a building, missile, lighthouse?

Then, I had a sense experience. I smelled, actually smelled, the room Tim and I lived in years ago at my former in-laws' residence. It was fascinating. Very vivid. I was aware of being in my own physical bed, but I could smell pecans, the electric heater, the enclosed, little-used storage smell. I could have been standing in the room, the aroma was so real and all-encompassing. What was funny was, I consciously didn't remember observing that smell in there before. As soon as the scent reached me, however, I knew that was where it had been, in that room, no other, eighteen years past and one hundred and fifty miles from here.

Reading, Brian, strangers, places in the house. Who were all of these people I was seeing and what was their significance? There was nothing unusual about them. They looked like perfectly ordinary people and places. Some of the places did have a brilliance, clarity and beauty somehow different from physical reality. I was still mystified by it all. There was no coherence, no cohesion to any of the Soul Sight images.

One day, I saw my entire body lying on the bed. I was not out of my body, but still in it, using my inner sight to view it from the perspective of my chin. The next day, in the middle of a "vision," I was able to manipulate my physical body. I opened my physical eyes while I was using Soul Sight. The scene I was "seeing" was still there, but now it was superimposed on the physical background of the room I was in.

As time went on I became more and more aware of my multi-dimensional, spiritual body. When I relaxed prior to most visions, I felt a portion of myself swaying back and forth in my physical body. I could only assume it was my spiritual body freeing itself from the physical.

On July 17th I was resting as usual, and various thoughts were floating through my mind. For some unknown reason, I was thinking of spaceships materializing in the sky. The noise from trucks passing outside my window bothered me, and I thought of our upcoming vacation to some supposedly beautiful red rock territory. All of a sudden...

I "saw"' two shimmering, colorful objects appear before me in the bright blue sky where the ceiling of my bedroom should have been. Though initially at quite a distance, they spun closer and turned into the shapes of trucks against a background of red stone mountains.

What a revelation! My thoughts had just materialized before me! I lay there hardly able to breathe. How could I have been so stupid? Of course! All the books said your thoughts materialize in the spirit environment! Why hadn't I realized this before now? My mind raced. Each thought clamored for attention. Berating myself, I realized some of the inexplicable was now explained. Was this why I "saw" my son so frequently? He was still a young child, and I always listened for sounds from him during my relaxation sessions and his naps. Was this the reason for my bird flight experience? Did I wonder, in this mutable spiritual environment, what it would be like to be a bird, and I became one?

I lay there wide-eyed letting this fact take further hold. I have evidently reached that level... area... state... plane... mode of consciousness... wherein thoughts are instantly transformed into objects or experiences. How could I have been so dense? I had read all of the infernal books. Logic came to my rescue. The brevity of the visions could be one explanation. They were always so darned short. The ignorance of the contents of my mind just prior to the use of Soul Sight was definitely another factor. *Thoughts became objects or experiences there!*

The implications of this fact became immediately apparent to me. If I were visiting a plane where thoughts materialize, I wanted to know what I was thinking! I didn't want to be unconsciously cast about. I had to admit, while I had been examining my beliefs and changing any unconstructive ones I encountered, thoughts had been allowed to flow, relatively freely. Well, not any more. They were more important than I imagined! I immediately began the practice of noting all thoughts which entered my mind.

Future Events

Because there are bleedthroughs and interconnections, it is possible for you to tune into a "future event", ... If so, such a dream is a message from a probable self who <u>did</u> experience the event.

Seth, Seth Speaks, *Session 566*

Preferring to read, I rarely watched television. I joined Brian and his favorite cartoons when he wanted my viewing company, but tonight, I was in the mood to watch some television. Glancing through the program listing, I stopped in amazement. "Good Grief!" I thought. "There is a movie on later tonight called Hester Street!" I recognized the name as that of the book from my Lydia/poetry dream three years ago. I never imagined it was an actual book! It had been made into a film by Midwest Film, Inc. After enjoying the cool autumn evening and relishing the star-kissed sunset beyond the cottonwood trees, I sat down to watch the movie.

A psychologically rich masterpiece, the movie depicted the adjustments a family of Jewish immigrants underwent when they moved to America at the turn of the century. The husband arrived first, and became an advocate of the new ways and mores of American life. Former restrictions imposed by his traditional Jewish dogma were discarded, and he became involved with a Polish woman who worked at a dance studio. When his wife and son joined him here, his wife refused to change her tradition, habits and beliefs as he requested. They eventually divorced and married others. He married the dancer and she married a devout, fundamentalist Jew.

It was a wonderful movie, and I was excited when it was over. My dream had been precognitive! Many of the elements of the dream were illustrated in the movie: Jews, a wedding, a dancer/prostitute, a remarriage, and the psychology of the difference in women. Mercy, I loved life! Throughout the months of record keeping I noticed that other precognitive dreams, equally vivid, held more personally relevant information.

The library was my destination. I was helping an imprisoned chained-by-the-ankle giant by getting some books for him to read. Once there, I was told, specifically, to read a book called *Alexandria* which was written by, or had something to do with, a psychic.

A little over a month later, feeling a mite silly but learning not to ignore these helpful impulses, I decided to check and see if the dream book existed. Looking in the local library card catalogue, I was surprised to find a book listed called the *Alexandria Project*. The book was about an archeologist's use of psychics to find ancient ruins in Alexandria, Egypt! I couldn't believe it. I immediately put my name on a waiting list to borrow the book. After several weeks on the list, I finally had to borrow the book from the University library.

I was quite pleased when I read it. Not only did it demonstrate successful use of psychic abilities, it also answered a question I had been pondering prior to the dream event. What were the practical benefits of psychic abilities? Evidently, archeology was one area psychic abilities were successfully used, and dreams, it seemed, could be quite informative.

69

Access to relevant physical material was something I never expected to find in the often incomprehensible dream state. Intuitive impulses, followed, also had their merit.

In another dream, our house was cracking, both the upstairs floor and the downstairs walls. It was indeed cracking, and leaking, as we discovered our son's upstairs bathroom carpet soaked one morning a little over a week later. Five years later, we discovered it had been true about the downstairs walls as well. While cleaning out a storage area under the stairs prior to moving, we found evidence of another leak, this time affecting the hidden downstairs storage walls. Only good record keeping and a concerted effort at dream recall allowed me to recognize these precognitive properties of the dream state.

One night I dreamt that I went against my intuition and drove to a freeway entrance that was still under construction. It was closed, and I had to turn around and go back. I was panic-stricken in the dream, but continued to my destination. A week later I was driving to meet my husband for lunch, the dream totally forgotten. I received an intuitive nudge to use a different route to reach him, but rationally rejected the idea and went my usual way. I became, literally, panic stricken when the freeway entrance I went to was closed and under construction. I had to backtrack and drive almost five miles out of my way to get on the freeway, all the while worried that I would be late for my lunch date!

Another time I was visiting my sister and her husband in the Philippines. They were having drainage problems with their house plumbing fixtures and I was helping them carry water in to alleviate the problems. In their mud-covered back yard was a small black dog.

About three weeks later, I received a letter from this sister, written about ten days before I had the dream. In it she spoke of Hurricane Gordon, which had gone through their area, and their having to catch rain water to flush their toilets! Two years later when we visited them, she showed me a picture of their little black dog! I had no prior knowledge that they had one.

Several times I was able to keep track of my first husband through my "dreams."

In one, he came to me and told me he was leaving the country for a while. In another "dream," I visited him and his new wife in the town and home in which they lived. She appeared to be part Spanish or Oriental.

More than two years later, I learned from a mutual friend that he had indeed left the country on a several-month-long sabbatical, had indeed married an Oriental woman, and was living right where the dream had designated.

When people appear to be sick in my dreams, I now begin to worry about them. Vivid dreams in which my brother, uncle and father-in-law were sick all preceded any knowledge of their illnesses and their imminent demises. Even a friend's breast augmentations were food for my dream life, long before I learned of her surgery.

Future events in dreams or the out-of-body state can be very specific. We *can* visit people or places in the future. In one dream, I was overlooking a fenced valley below an orchard. Near the orchard were three goats. At the time of the dream, I couldn't figure out why I was there or why I would be dreaming of goats. I was living in a large desert city; active and happy in that lifestyle. Over seven years later when my husband retired, we moved to the Pacific Northwest.

Our lifestyle changed completely when we purchased a home in the country which quite coincidentally looked out over a valley below an orchard. Next to that orchard live three goats. Though the dream goats were interwoven in dream elements, I know this was the valley I visited in my dream.

My favorite future-event dream was totally awe-inspiring and reflected the true miracle of the reality in which we live.

I dreamt I was attending a baby shower and was playing with a curly, dark-haired baby. The baby had quite a distinct head of hair. I was playing with her for some time in the dream, and there was something about the number three I was supposed to remember, but which eluded me.

The dream didn't surprise me, as I was to attend a baby shower later that evening. When I went to the shower, several guests arrived late, one of whom had a baby with her. I didn't know the woman, that she had a child, or that any children would be at the shower. The baby was the Baby from my dream! I almost fainted! There was no mistake about it. She was a *three*-month-old little girl, but appeared to be much older because of the tremendous shock of thick black hair that covered her head. Never had I felt more blessed. The moments were sacred as I played with the future-event baby.

Getting Out

*The "inner" body can perform in ways that the
physical body cannot, and you can use that as a
challenge. Find out what you can do with your inner
body; experiment.*

Seth, The Unknown Reality, *Vol. 1, Session 683*

My life continued as usual. I was a busy housekeeper, mother, wife, and community volunteer. Extremely happy in my roles, somehow I still found time to "travel" and learn. I soon discovered, for instance, the property of instant materialization explained many of the events I experienced in the out-of-body environment, but it didn't explain all of them. There were times during the use of Soul Sight when I was not thinking anything at all, and I would experience things.

My inner body, for example, often came into my Soul Sight awareness *without* prior thought causing such a materialization. Oftentimes, I would just become aware of it doing something. I would sense my hands, or see my face, or be floating over my physical body, looking down on it. Once I even noticed my inner toes playfully crossing themselves! Something I could never have done physically, nor would even think of doing.

At times, I would find myself in various areas of our home or portions of our yard. I would not sense a body, but the "I-ness" of me, the conscious portion of myself, would be aware of being beside a piece of household furniture, or a physical tree or bush.

One September afternoon, while relaxing and using Soul Sight, I saw an expanse of land with rolling sand-dune shapes outlined by desert plants. Though not uncommon in the southwest desert, this was a beautiful vista, and I managed to get a longer look at it. While admiring the view, I decided to turn to the right to see what was in that direction. Upon doing so, I saw a big, gabled, maroon house. Looking down on the sprawling place, I couldn't figure out why it had several fireplace chimneys.

Physically, days later, I took a new route to deliver Brian to preschool. I almost drove off the road. There were the sand dunes and the "house!" Since I was last on this street, maroon townhouses had been built one quarter mile from our home. Each townhouse had a fireplace, and several connected units were built at this time. To the left of these buildings was an unobstructed view of the mesas I had seen.

I had definitely been out of body, in the air, outdoors when my Soul Sight showed me this view. It was *not* a thought manifestation. This place existed physically, and I had seen it from the air. I had been out of body, floating, unaware of a body, seeing the physical environment. The Soul Sight environment was a definite environment from which physical reality could be viewed. Though thoughts *could* manifest there, it was still a *place* I was visiting, and not a mere function of my mind.

Not long after this realization, I tried a new technique to get consciously OOB. I reassured myself that it was perfectly safe and easy to be OOB, and I imagined myself being out. I visualized myself standing at the opposite end of the room. After nine days of trying this technique, I succeeded. For a few seconds, I saw myself. Me looking at me. The physical me was fully clothed lying on the bed, the spiritual me was standing *naked* at the foot of the bed! Seeing myself was somewhat of a shock to my physical body.

When I came back to my body, my heart was pounding in fright. I had definitely not visualized myself naked. I had succeeded, though not in the way I assumed I would.

As I analyzed the situation, I became quite angry. What was I afraid of? Were my fears inhibiting my ability to explore this environment? Was that why my OOBE's were so brief? I got up in a huff. My disgust at myself and my possible inadequacies were quite strong. I would change my beliefs. I live in a completely safe universe, and if I weren't meant to explore the OOB environment, then I wouldn't have been made aware of it. My determination rose. I would not be held back by fears, physically or spiritually.

Loving

True spirituality is a thing of joy and of the earth, and has nothing to do with fake adult dignity. It has nothing to do with long words and sorrowful faces. It <u>has</u> to do with the dance of consciousness that is within you, and with the sense of spiritual adventure that is within your hearts.

Seth, Seth Speaks, *Appendix*

Cleaning utensils in their bucket... setting those down lovingly... separating the blue and white sheets... sending love to them... oh... ah... sending love to my back... which just gave me a pain... towels, big towels, print shirt, more sheets, my "I Must Be Dreaming" nightshirt... thanking All That Is for creating all this for my use.

Realizing that all consciousness... that all things have consciousness... that love is the strongest force there is... thanking the liquid detergent for being itself...transmitting love to the clothes washer... thanking it for being such a help to me over the years... transmitting the love mentally... with my whole body.

Feeling the cold tile against my bare feet... opening the refrigerator door... thanking it... loving it... sending it my love and thanks... picking up the cold Coke can... opening it... thanking it... loving it... knowing it will nourish my body... taking a drink... feeling the wetness flow down my throat... replacing the can in the refrigerator... heading up the stairs to begin my household cleaning... walking over the carpet... feeling the soft springiness... gripping the cold, gold doorknob of the linen closet... opening the door... sending it love... removing clean sheets from the shelf... sending them love... noticing the graceful movements of my body... feeling the rhythm of... love.

Noticing the beauty... of the sheets... transmitting love... caressing the sheets of the just-made bed... noticing the morning light enhancing the sheets, merging with the sheets... running my hand along the bed... putting on the comforter... straightening it out... noticing the fluffiness of the feather pillows as I put on the clean pillowcases... transmitting love... thanking them for cradling our heads over the years.

Walking into the bathroom... turning on the water faucet... feeling the rag fill with moisture... feeling the wetness of my hands... noticing my hands... looking at the miracle of them... loving them... washing the toilet with the rag and scouring powder... slowly... slowly... sending love... hoping the animate and inanimate objects receive it... hoping they realize I sincerely mean it... flushing the toilet... listening to it gurgle down the pipes.

Wiping the shelf... cleaning off the dust... wiping my magic bottle... a gift Bob gave me... sending it love... whenever I open it I am to make a wish... and the genie, the magical self, grants my wish... thanking him for that... dusting the other knickknacks... all the crevices... and I thank them for their beauty... a powder-blue porcelain bottle that fits in the palm of my hand... the cork falls out... inside are lilac petals from my first blossoms... I marvel at the sacredness of them... I send them love.

I begin washing the mirrors... sending love as my hand swirls around the mirror... moving in wide arches and little circles... marveling at how clearly the mirror reflects objects... me... I could be on the other side of that mirror, another me... it is so clear... I look at myself in the mirror... no makeup on... hair a mess... loving myself... no matter how imperfect I appear to be... my god-self exists in that reflection.

Finishing the bathroom... sending love... moving into the sitting room... dusting the book shelves... the television... sending love... picking up a tin box with a picture of a little boy sitting on a bed smiling at an elf... the caption reads Believing Is Seeing... sending love... holding a card I once gave Bob... the front of which reads I Love You, I Love You, I Love You, I Love You, I Love You, I Love You, I Love You... in a rainbow of colors... the inside says... What More Can I Say?

My day continued this way. For ten hours I concentrated in the Present and noticed only what was before me. Recognizing and acknowledging the godliness of all life. Thanking whatever I encountered, animate or not, for being in my life. After dinner I walked into the living room. As I stood there, about to sit in a recliner, I left my body. I was *out of body while totally conscious and physically active.*

My physical body finished my intended movement by sitting in the chair. My consciousness hovered in the air beside the chair. When I realized what had happened, I vigorously shook my physical head, which brought me, my consciousness, back into the physical body, and I let out an exclamation of surprise. Will wonders never cease?!

Energy Transfers

*Such multi-dimensional symbols will appear then in
many ways, not simply visually. They will affect not
only your own physical reality, but all realities in
which you are involved.*

Seth, Seth Speaks, *Session 572*

I dreamt I was going to college and was
rooming with at least two other girls. I was
going through some used clothes that
someone had given me. I noticed that against the
wall above our heads we each had a clear cylinder
that held a liquid. One girl's was all reddish, and the
other's was multicolored. This liquid shimmered, like
champagne bubbles, in various colors. One girl
commented to the other that she had plenty of liquid,
and that it appeared that the other one hadn't used
much of hers. She felt she needed to cleanse herself
more.

I observed this exchange, then was by my dream
bed looking out the window to see what kind of view I
had. When I looked out I could see a tunnel with
men traversing it. It looked like this was the way men
were to come. Instantaneously, I was out by a
mailbox, and two men were heading for our room. I
also returned and joined what appeared to be some
kind of initiation ceremony. The other girls were
given different positions in which to stand - like
statues. I was handed a clear, round, crystal vase
with a pure white flower in it. I brought the vase to

my chest and looked at the face-size flower. It was indescribably gorgeous, with unique individual flowerettes within the larger flower. I was so overcome by the beauty of the flower that I started to show it to the man next to me, when Brian woke me up.

The energy I felt upon awakening was tremendous. I was suffused with love and awe. The dream had been extremely vivid, and the elements of the dream, breathtaking. The dream elements, in this case, appeared to be symbolic. Though the events seem chaotic and illogical from our point of view, they are completely logical according to the rules of the dream state.

The "reality" behind such powerful dreams seems inexplicable, but according to those who know, the feelings experienced during and after these dreams are what are important. The feeling imparted by this dream was not only one of awe but that I had reached some heretofore unknown depth of my soul. It was as if I had been imparted some knowledge, possibly on the cellular level, which was incomprehensible to me intellectually. Some multi-dimensional truths, it appears, can only be grasped by a three-dimensionally focused human through the use of symbols.

The symbols are true on many levels of reality but the "mail," or message, I interpreted from this dream was that I am one of the small, beautiful flowers within the larger flower (All That Is). I was in school (earth) and the tunnel was the path men (humans) had to follow to get where they were going - to learn, to create, or to play. I was happy for hours after this dream. The impact and the energy transfer were literally astounding.

Another dream found me in my unknown kitchen, looking through the door at flowers that were in my indoor garden/greenhouse. I entered the area, drawn by the beauty of the flowers. When I noticed some I didn't recognize, I tried to focus closer on them. They were a row of foot-high plants with large, absolutely stunning, pink-orange leaves on them. Standing there, I worried how they would be pollinated indoors.

At that moment, a beautiful hand-size (length) monarch-type butterfly flew in the open door of the house. Huge and magnificently beautiful, it flew around the room. It fluttered over to the door it had entered, but it didn't fly out. I decided I wanted a picture of it and asked Bob to get the camera. When I turned back, it was now a child-size butterfly, or rather, a child with wings!! Then, as I looked closer, beyond all reasoning, a child without wings!

The child's mother was outside looking for her child. She was a beautiful woman-size, black butterfly. Or rather, a woman with black wings. She was carrying what appeared to be a girl's white dress with puffy sleeves. Bob had returned and was taking pictures of the child and its wings. The child's mother was relieved to learn her child was in our home. She came in and consented to have her picture taken as well.

The camera was now out of film, so Bob went to get his other camera. The mother wanted to leave, as it had started to rain just as she came in the house. At this time, a white-winged grandmother entered the house. They could somehow make their wings disappear. You could only see two scars on their backs where the wings had once been. Bob returned, and the beings started posing with their wings for us. Shortly afterward, they left.

No words can even begin to describe the wonder and awe I felt during this dream and after I awoke. These types of experiences, in some inexplicable way, generally realign your psychological sense of self and well-being. They seem to balance your essence while they simultaneously thrill you and lavish you with more energy. Another similar energy transfer was evident in this next dream.

I was in line registering to take some classes, greeting people I knew. I was filling out a form of colored circles that corresponded to the different times the classes were held. As I was concentrating on the colored circles, I was spontaneously transported to another dreamscape. The new dreamscape was one in which I was gazing into a basket filled with precious stones. I was filled with wonder as I gazed at the sparkling gems. I was soon distracted when a Wild Woman came into the room.

Short, dark, spiky unkempt hair crowned her weathered face. Half naked, she stood before me, power emanating from every pore of her body. She and several other women had baskets filled with the precious stones. The gems were considered valuable to us. The Wild Woman had a purple one, and was showing it to another girl who was somehow connected to me (as if she were a former self, reincarnation, of me). She didn't look anything like me. She had long, dark hair, and reminded me of an East Indian woman.

There were rugs on the dirt floors, and we may have been in some kind of hut. The Wild Woman wanted the other me to pick a stone from one of the baskets. They wanted me to pick a red one, but I chose a purple one. It was a little bigger than a quarter, and flat. There was some connection to its being worn, or useful, in relation to the Third Eye area.

Then I woke up from this very vivid, very real dream. Wonder and awe again accompanied this experience. What was interesting was that while the dream woman offered the stone to the other me, I felt like I was the one who had chosen the stone; as if I had moved into and become, or merged with, this other me. Yet I still retained my sense of identity. I was surprised by the implication of the dream that there was another me who looked entirely different from me, but was still somehow me. This was indicative to me that if reincarnation did exist in a simultaneous time period, then we often accessed each others' experiences. As part of a whole identity of incarnational selves, experience could be and was, most often unknowingly to be sure, shared by all parts (incarnations) related to the same source-entity.

Quite often some of my short dreams held an equally energizing impact. These were solid experiences in that I "knew" what I had been doing prior to awakening, but few details remained of the dream content or specific dream actions. For instance, one time I awoke from visiting a place where one could automatically create physical objects. I couldn't remember the details, but I knew this was where I had been and what I had been doing. In a similar dream experience, I awoke knowing I had just planted a seed for the Tree of Life.

Another time, I "dreamt" only voices. This was unusual as it was extremely real and un-dream-like. It felt as if I were confronting some tribunal, or authority figure. I was asked the question, "What are you searching for?" I answered, "The Law." The voice then asked, "What will you do when you find it?" I answered with much conviction, "Live It."

Lucidity

[After death] Now there is an in-between stage of relative indecision, a midplane of existence; a rest area, comparatively speaking, and it is from this area that most communications from relatives occurs. This is usually the level that is visited by the living in projections from the dream state.

Seth, Seth Speaks, *Chap. 11*

My dreams began to elicit tactile sense phenomena. I had been experiencing vivid dreams for some time, but now I noticed instances in dreams where I became consciously aware of the dream environment. I was no longer merely observing dream events unfold, or remembering them, I was *in the dreams consciously experiencing the dream events*. Once lucid, the dream events became as real as physical reality.

After experiencing a few of these, I was able to recognize what appeared to cause these new phenomena. A vivid dream, I found, was transformed into a lucid dream by various factors. Intellectual curiosity often prompted it. For instance, once I was dreaming of a being/man that could adopt any shape or form it wanted. I was seeing a swirling mass of small, colorful "bubbles" changing shape. My interest became piqued and I tried to get a better look at the phenomenon. As I did so, the experience became immediate. I automatically, with no conscious decision other than my curiosity and desire, projected into the dreamscape and I *was* standing inside the dream watching these beautiful lights transform the being's overall shape.

I was filled with wonder as I concentrated in the dreamscape and after I awoke (returned to my physical body) from it. The shift in states of consciousness from being an observer of the dream as we usually think of it to being consciously inside the dream was obvious. Fluid, easy, immediate, but a definite shift of presence into and out of a dream drama.

Often some odd dream occurrence would trigger lucidity in a dream. Like the time I joined a party being held in a stunning indoor/outdoor area.

The pristine grounds were filled with people dressed in elegant evening clothes. I consciously became aware in the dream when I focused my attention on some birds. The birds were trained or willingly flew down to pick at the women's bright skirts. As birds gracefully swooped among the laughing guests, the scene was rendered quite enchanting. After watching this shimmering, gay scene for a while, I asked someone for directions to leave, and following them, entered an elevator in a nearby building.

The elevator doors opened on the 8th floor, and I saw unbelievably beautiful, round, five-foot-tall, colored lights hovering in the air. This is difficult to describe, but beauty, love, and energy emanated from these lights. The door closed and we continued upward. On the next floor was an awe-inspiring mosaic hallway, subtly lighted, with lightning zigzag designs on the hallway doors. The atmosphere was electrifying, and was as real and gorgeous as it could possibly be. Then somebody, an unseen companion, I assume, commented that his chosen route, the one we were on, had been better than the way I would have taken. I couldn't argue with that.

Birds in dreams often triggered lucidity for me. One night I dreamt ...

I was at a family reunion being held at a resort area. I was, at first, in a small enclosed entranceway of a house. I became totally aware, totally present when I noticed a hummingbird in the room with me. I ignored it and looked out the back screen door at the beautiful landscape. There seemed to be some kind of barrier to keep the birds (something?) away from the plants (living things?), but I couldn't see what the barrier was. Vague as this sounds, I just "knew" something would, given the chance, destroy something that needed to be protected.

I turned away from the door and noticed a tawny speckled bird in the room with me. I picked him up. He clung tightly to my hand, wrapping his feet around it, and did not want to let go! I held it for a while, gaining complete tactile sensations from the bird. In other words, I could feel the bird's feet as if I were physically holding it and not holding it in a dream. I opened the door and set him on the ground where he promptly grabbed onto a bug to protect me from it. I then went out into the resort grounds. I walked among the trees and flowers for quite a while and returned to the house when I became hungry.

I entered a kitchen/dining room area and saw my deceased grandmother, my father's mother. She looked perfectly normal, vital, and was doing what she always loved doing while alive, preparing food for others. Surprised, I continued up a nearby staircase and passed through a room filled with other deceased relatives. This was really uncanny. I knew they were dead, but there they were, alive and functioning in what appeared to me as a very real environment.

My father, who had died partially paralyzed, was standing across the room from me. Apparently completely healed and appearing much younger than when he had died, he was looking the other way from me as I passed by. An Aunt, physically still alive, appeared to be blind. She was lying on a bed, one arm outstretched, requesting aid from someone. I was shocked by her appearance. She looked terrible. (What was strange, several years after this "dream," I saw a photograph of this particular Aunt, and was again appalled by her appearance. She looked like an entirely different person from when I knew her. Life had really changed her in the twenty-five years since I had last seen her.) I continued walking through the room in the dream and encountered another recently deceased Uncle. Again I was startled by this. He was sitting on the edge of a bed, talking to his daughter. He asked her why she had such a sad face. She told him it was because she had just lost her father (him), and they hugged. The "dream" ended.

Did I actually visit my deceased relatives? Was it real? If you do believe in life after death, then loved ones would have to exist somewhere until they chose their next courses of action. My dream scenario could be as true as any other. I know it certainly felt as real and solid as physical reality.

Another time before I went to sleep, I told myself I would take my "aware" self with me wherever I went in my dreams, and this is what happened.

I told Bob I would meet him at the Holland Tunnel. I was concerned that we would pass each other, as we would be coming from opposite directions. I became lucid at the tunnel, dodging the traffic, when I saw Bob in his suit, crossing the street and coming for me. Reassured at the sight of him, I reached a small indentation in the tunnel near the entrance. Knowing Bob would soon be joining me, I ran out of that small area to a nearby building. The men's room door was around the corner to my left. While waiting, I leaned against some pipes or junction boxes. Suddenly, I heard music coming from a circular stairwell which led downwards. Strangely drawn to the music, I walked over to the stairs. Above the stairwell entranceway was a sign which read "Living." I became confused and woke up.

As fascinating as these and other similar lucid experiences were, I still was encountering problems with my main interest - getting out of body. I sincerely wanted to experience this. While I frequently used Soul Sight (had, in fact, recorded eighty-nine times of such use in 1989), actually being completely out of body, aware of a spiritual body, and in complete control of where I was and what I was doing, still eluded me.

False Awakening

The art of dreaming is a <u>science</u> long forgotten by your world. Such an art, pursued, trains the mind in a new kind of consciousness - one that is equally at home in either existence, well-grounded and secure in each.

Seth, The Unknown Reality, *Vol. 1, Session 700*

I lay back in bed. Brian was still wiggling beside me, trying to get comfortable. It was his nap time. He was five now, in kindergarten, but he still needed a nap to defer grumpiness later in the day due to fatigue. I had lain with him to help him get to sleep. I thought of how busy our lives had become since he started school. I volunteered at his school when they needed help with parties or special events, and we were getting out more. We had introduced Brian to team sports and he loved them.

As I relaxed, my physical eyes closed, I "saw" Brian's sweat-soaked red back. I reminded myself to write it down later, then continued trying to go to sleep. A nap was just what I needed. My arms kept becoming numb, though, and waking me up. I was accustomed to my waterbed, not Brian's standard mattress. I kept drifting off and being reawakened. I was becoming quite irritated when Brian woke up. He began playing with the telephone and the radio, so I decided I may as well get up, as I would receive no more rest. He walked to our bedroom and I joined him in there.

I turned off the radio in the master bedroom and

went back to Brian's room while he remained waiting for me in the hall. He yelled that the mailman was at the door. As I went downstairs, I looked out the window and saw a blue truck next to the door. In the entranceway on the first floor, I noticed two floor tiles were broken near the door. An unknown man was fixing them. He nodded at me, I returned the nod, and turned to go into the kitchen, but it was not our kitchen!

There was a dark board over the door with carved curlicues on it. I entered the kitchen, walked straight ahead toward a stove/counter area with cups hanging over it. When I saw it, I thought, "How pretty," and *knew consciously* I wasn't in our house as it was now.

I was about to sit down, when my mother, who was there along with a good friend, asked me to let the neighbor lady sit there. I acquiesced, picked up a tablet from the table, sat down in another seat, and started writing all these surprising events down. The neighbor's daughter was there also, but she was only about three or four years old. The daughter was actually my age, but I let that pass. My step-father and Bob were present as well. They were in a raised living room area (where our dining room would be in physical reality) which had a fireplace and two sofas, one on either side of it.

One sofa was blue, the other brown. I then realized that when I had walked down the stairs earlier, someone had been fixing the tiles by the door, and there was nothing wrong with ours. I realized, again, that I was either dreaming or OOB. I decided that if I were OOB, I needed to write this in waking reality, not this one. I thought of my body, forced myself awake, and wrote this account.

Wow, that was strange! Just as real as it could possibly be, yet in a dreamscape. During the day that this had happened, I noted in my journal that Bob had received a raise in salary, I had written more on my precognitive dream anthology, I had talked to a sister long distance the night before, and listened to Beethoven with Brian. So, my travels into the dream/OOB environment were not adversely affecting my normal, waking existence. About six days later, I was again napping with Brian when another "dream" happened.

I was awakened by a blue pickup truck dropping someone off in our driveway. I drifted back to sleep. Later, when it was time to get up, I was having a difficult time waking up, but I finally managed it. Brian woke up as well and we were playing in his room for a while, laughing and giggling, before he climbed onto my back to be carried downstairs. I walked out of the bedroom with Brian, when I saw something drop to the hall floor from the wall. It looked like a lizard. When it saw us, it sprang up on the wall like a spider monkey. Startled, I looked closer and discovered it was a tiger! Somewhat panicked, I set Brian down and told him to run downstairs, open the door, and run to safety, while I grabbed some hangers from a closet. As Brian obeyed, the tiger jumped from the wall and started to follow him. The tiger was whiter now, and smaller, like a baby tiger. Reacting immediately, I threw some hangers at it to distract it. Brian escaped, whereupon the tiger turned toward me, or at least to the hangers on the floor. It was a full-sized striped tiger again!

With Brian safe, all of the bewildering events caused logic to begin to surface. I wondered why the entrance in the hallway looked different and why there were hangers already on the floor, before I had thrown mine. I kept trying to wake up and couldn't. I heard voices outdoors and saw the back of a boy scout through the hall window. He was talking to someone outside of my view. I remembered the "dream" I just had and thought that Brian was too short to have reached in my purse for the door keys. I reminded myself to move them. Then(!), I finally managed to wake up physically.

Good God, I had just had another false-awakening dream! There is no better description for it. These are dreams in which you think you have awakened and are going about your business, when actually you are still in the dreamscape representation of physical reality. The events seem totally real, but your full critical faculties are not quite functioning in that environment yet. In this one, I was thoroughly convinced I was awake and playing with my son, and yet I had *reacted to* the tiger instead of realizing that there was no tiger in my home!

When this "dream" occurred, I had been finding it difficult to wake up during the previous few days. I felt I was either trying to animate a corpse or a dream image. Two months later, as I was writing another dream, I realized I was *still dreaming*, and had to wake myself to write it physically. In August I decided that the best technique to use to get OOB would be to awaken myself in my dreams and travel from that state wherever I wanted to go, whatever time, place, or dimension that appealed to me. On the 30th, before I went to sleep, I told myself I would realize I was dreaming and would travel.

I dreamt I was dreaming, and woke up. I woke Bob for some reason, by tapping him on the shoulder, then he did the same to me. He jumped on me, shaking and teasing me, several times. That confused me. Why was he trying to wake me up when I was already awake? Then I thought I heard Brian call out, and went to check on him. As I did, I passed a beige cat in our bedroom doorway, and thought, "What is that cat doing here?" When I got to Brian's room, *Bob* was lying there with him, and Rema, one of our dead cats, was on top of Bob, licking his face! Sammie, another of our deceased cats, was lying on the bed beside them. Brian was okay, and I thought of waking Bob to tell him about the cats. Then I finally realized I was still dreaming, a false awakening dream, and I returned to and entered my body. I could sense my spiritual body moving back and forth trying to animate my physical body. Once my spiritual body was aligned with the physical body, I roused myself physically and recorded what had happened.

I felt wide awake in this dream, as if it were physical reality. I was just confused at the strange events.

I was quite happy that my pre-sleep suggestion had worked. I felt somewhat concerned that my total critical self still wasn't alert enough to rid me of the thought forms or dream elements, however. Reasoning further, I realized that the cats didn't necessarily have to be thought forms. While OOB, others had used the technique of wishing away the appearance of anything that was not usually a part of the normal physical environment. If the image disappeared, it was considered a manifestation of the unconscious mind; if it didn't, it was part of the OOB environment. So the cats may, or may not, have been real in that spiritual environment.

Full of Life

The true [mental] physicist will be a bold explorer - not picking at the universe with small tools, but allowing his consciousness to flow into the many open doors that can be found with no instrument, but with the mind.

Seth, The Unknown Reality, *Vol. 1, Session 701*

I was floating... floating... aware rather than dreaming. I was practicing getting out of my body and knew I could do it. Knew I was out. Then someone—all I could see was a hand and part of a forearm—poured something from a drawstring medicine bag onto the bed. On the pink blanket were what looked like two green bugs. Oval shaped. Big for bugs. With light green speckles on their backs. I saw one of them move and wanted a closer look. As I leaned over the bed and focused, I noticed one bug had wings--like butterfly wings--in pinks, but it flew away. The other one had yellow wings that were folded and attached... to a tiny person!!!

I literally jumped for joy. My god, it was a fairy! Quite elated, I tried to get close to it. It flew into the air, and I began chasing it around the room to get a better look at it. The tiny fairies seemed both shy and full of fun. I probably scared the daylights out of them, but they were way too fast for that to be much of a concern. Zipping around the room, the one I was chasing hid behind the door, then got out to the balcony and flew off. I lost track of the other one. I have never been so thrilled in my life! My whole soul, being, brightened during this experience.

I will never forget the tiny fairies, and I will always treasure the experience of meeting them while OOB. Whatever you want to call it, the event was real while it was happening.

When Nature was beginning to awaken its sleeping landscape in March 1991, I had an intriguing false-awakening dream.

I "dreamt" I was wondering what time it was and if I should get up from my nap. Brian and Bob came over to see if I was up, an alarm clock went off to wake me, and someone came to the window to wake me. So, with all of the disturbances, I roused myself, looked out the window and saw a red 4x4 truck floating near my second-story bedroom window. When I couldn't figure that out, I turned and started walking out of the room. As I was walking along the carpet, I noticed myself thinking, "Wouldn't it be neat if it took me a long time to get to the door?" And that is what I immediately experienced.

It seemed like it took me eons, ages, millennia to get to the door of the bedroom. This is very difficult to describe, but time stretched. Literally, centuries seemed to pass as I walked to the door. The sensation ceased as soon as I reached the door, and I returned to a normal time sequence. Then, as I was descending the stairs, another unusual thought surfaced, "What if I were a tiny person trying to get to the edge of that step?" And that is what I experienced. I *felt* tiny and experienced the walk to the edge of the stairs as if I were traversing a vast distance. From my perspective as a tiny person, the space was elongated. I walked and walked and walked. Once I reached the edge of the step, I returned to normal size; downstairs, I could see Bob talking to a man I didn't know but who looked familiar. He was about fifty years old, blonde, thin, and wore eyeglasses. He gave me a strange, evaluating look while Bob showed him his belt. They began talking about lawn sprinklers. I left them with their discussion and returned to physical reality.

As soon as I was back I began to analyze what I had just experienced. As far as this experience was concerned, physically Bob was home, sick and sleeping with Brian. It could have been some aspects of Brian and Bob unconsciously present with me OOB. I wasn't able to place the unknown man. He was no one I knew consciously. Since Bob was asleep, could I have entered a dream he was having?

The facet I found extremely interesting was how time factored into this OOBE. I was wondering about the current time and began experiencing different aspects, different perspectives of the time/space concept. Powerful sensations indeed. I shook my head in wonder and smiled at the unbelievable complexity of the true human condition and environment.

In September, I went up to relax while Bob played outdoors with Brian. Being somewhat tired, within minutes I was OOB.

I seemed to be experiencing other realities, counterparts to physical reality. It was as if I could switch from any reality and experience the one I chose. I couldn't seem to find the right one, and was hovering over myself, spiritually slapping myself in the physical face to wake myself.

I was beginning to get very nervous, when I saw a cigarette, which distracted me. I thought it might be nice to experience a reality in which I smoked, since I had recently quit physically. Acknowledging my desire for a cigarette, I thought, metaphorically, that the floor had fallen out from under me when I quit. I had always enjoyed smoking.

The next thing I knew, Brian, Bob and I were in the upstairs hallway leading to the staircase. Bob was hanging a picture on the wall and I was enjoying a cigarette, when the hallway floor fell out from under us! Bob tumbled off onto the lower floor, while Brian was hanging over the side, his head through the railing. They weren't hurt and quickly reached safety, but I was still hanging there, trying to scramble to safety and walk on the tilted floor. This was as real as real can be. My ashtray fell, and I screamed to the boys that it was coming.

I then realized I was "dreaming," that this wasn't my reality. I no longer smoked and definitely no longer wanted to experience that event. I forced myself awake, and lay there letting my heartbeat return to normal.

God, that was real. With my heart still pounding from the frightening experience, I was frustrated at my inability to recognize my true circumstances. How can these experiences feel so completely real, if they're not? Sighing as the calm and stable conditions of physical reality revived my spirits, I lay there thinking. Barely knowing how to interpret this experience, I decided that if what my "dream" said were true and there are parallel realities, I had better send that other "me" strength, courage, love, and peace. I did and imagined her making it off the damaged floor safely.

Several weeks later, in November, I was relaxing and just "floating" when...

I decided I should get up. But I was having trouble moving my body. It was as if a huge weight were on my chest. I began to panic, when I thought I heard Bob come in downstairs. But I knew he was at work. Then I heard what seemed to be Brian, but he was in school. So with great difficulty, I managed to stumble out of bed. Now up, I discovered I had a splitting headache and decided to go back to bed to try and make it go away. I returned to my body and realized that I hadn't physically arisen earlier.

I had been OOB, but was again sensing the environment as being physically real! What a shock this was! I still couldn't comprehend why it wouldn't be different somehow. Toward the end of the month, I found another clue to my experiences.

During the day when both my son and husband were gone, I had a vision using Soul Sight, then "dreamt" of myself being in bed and floating in and out of my body. There were many noises going on. Jackhammers were being used somewhere, motorcycles were going by outdoors, construction workers were hammering on wood, the radio was on and I was listening to people talking on it. I reached over physically to turn off the radio, *and it wasn't on*.

I finally decided these were all attempts created by my psyche to make me conscious that I was in the OOB state. I would have sworn, though, that all the noises were actually happening physically.

Despite all of the confusion caused by the perception that the OOB environment was the physical one, and the innumerable questions I wanted answered, I did find one key to successful OOBEs. The timing of my relaxation sessions was important. I needed one to two hours of complete quiet, with no chance of interruptions and no unfinished chores bothering my conscience, to reach the OOB plane. With this knowledge, I began using my time judiciously to that end. In January 1992 I did it. I had my first controlled OOB experience.

Control

*Molecular structures send out their own messages,
and unless you are tuned in to perceive them, they
may be interpreted as static or meaningless noise.
Any one of these levels of consciousness can be
covered in a twinkling, and no notice taken of it; or, at
least theoretically, you could spend a lifetime
exploring any given level.*

Seth, Seth Speaks, *Session 575*

I was resting, totally relaxed, and became
aware of my inner body swaying back and
forth as if I were resting on a cloud. I
recognized the sensation. It was one which preceded
most of my visions. I knew I was loose from the
physical, so I decided to try and lift out.

I could hear a rattling noise like paper being
crumpled. As I listened more closely to determine
what was making the sound, it became static, like on
a radio which wasn't tuned in properly, then actual
radio music. I could "see" the room with my Soul
Sight. My physical eyes were closed, so I tried to get
up spiritually. I popped out, and back in. I tried
again with the same result. Out and in. Out and in. I
didn't know what the problem was.

I lay there wondering what to do. Then a thought
entered my mind. If I just think of sitting up and
hold that image, maybe that will work. So I did, and
it did, and I was sitting up in my spiritual body
consciously aware that I was doing so. I became

quite excited. God, I'd finally done it! I went back in and thought of writing this account. I reached for a pad and pencil. I then thought, "No, now that I can get out, I'm going to explore." So I tried to stand. I imagined myself standing, then was literally doing so. I walked, using my spiritual body, toward the door of the room until I heard an unaccountable noise.

Concerned, I stopped, returned and entered my physical body and listened. When I heard no further noises, I tried to vacate my body again. I thought of how I wanted to be out, but that I didn't want to float. I didn't want my feet in the air.

The next thing I knew, my spiritual body, feet, shot straight up in the air, with my shoulders on the bed. I lay there, startled, in this precarious position, wondering what on earth! Somehow I had managed to think myself into that position! As my spiritual body automatically returned into my body, I lay there for a while wondering what to do, when suddenly, I saw the most beautiful eyes right in front of my face. They were a stunning blue, like in a lovely child's face.

I didn't know what I was seeing. I thought it was a fairy; then, no, maybe it was my own eyes I was looking at, but mine are green. It was like a reflection seen in a pane of glass. Then I heard a soft, extremely feminine voice whisper, as though not to frighten me, "So, how did you like that?"

At these words, I became uneasy. I decided that was enough for one day. I started moving my body back and forth, slapping my face with my spiritual hands and wiggling my physical form, to return to physicality.

I noticed, with some incomprehension upon reentering, that my physical arms were still beside my body as I had originally left them. It was so difficult to imagine that I hadn't actually been using my physical hands while out! I immediately reached for the notepad and pencil I had placed on the bed during the OOBE, and they weren't there! They must have been a thought-form.

I retrieved my pen and 8 x 11 inch notebook from the bedside table. In the OOBE, the pad had been a small hand-size notepad, and the pen had been a pencil. I quickly wrote all I had experienced, and reflected. I didn't know where the blue eyes came from nor who could have spoken to me. I didn't remember thinking the blue eyes and voice into existence. In fact, I was sure I hadn't. I kept a close watch on my thoughts these days, and was almost always aware what thoughts were in my mind. All things considered, it was a very successful venture. Although, I smiled, laughing at myself, there must be a more graceful way to re-animate the physical body!

As I lay there recalling the experience, I was suffused with pleasure at my success. I had done it! A truly controlled, more or less, self-initiated OOBE. It had taken me a long time and a lot of patience, but I had done it. Success comes in different forms for many people, I realized. If I never do anything else in life, if I am never rich nor famous nor respected, if I never achieve any other socially-defined success, I had done this. Nothing besides my husband and son had ever thrilled me more.

In April, I lay down about 11:30 in the morning. I had just taken two painkillers for a lower backache, and was just trying to get comfortable. While lying there, I noticed, felt or heard, a couple of snaps at the base of my neck. I thought good, maybe I'm making some physical adjustments to what I thought was a pinched nerve. I had no thoughts of OOBEs; I just wanted a nap.

After relaxing, just floating for a while, I decided I should get up to take a shower. It felt so good to float that I had considerable trouble convincing myself to stop. I finally rose and went downstairs into the kitchen. I took some clothes out of the clothes dryer. There were some of Brian's socks, and Bob's white shirt, and a gray leisure pullover. They were clinging together with static electricity, and I decided to take them to the ironing hamper in the den. As I was passing through the living room, I noticed dirt all around the base of the sofa.

I became aware that it had evidently sunk in, so I got on my knees and started moving the dirt from the higher end of this five inch trench, to the lower, sunken-in portion. I was filling it in when all of a sudden I felt extremely tired. Just exhausted. I lay back on the floor to rest for a moment and thought to myself, "Wouldn't it be funny if I were OOB and still upstairs in bed." Then, just like that, I *was* back in my physical body, in bed, aware of the physical again.

After writing the events, I lay there in bed contemplating. It appears that any thought of my body returns me right to it... which is good, I thought. The OOB elements puzzled me, though. Today was not washday, and there were no real clothes in my dryer. I was too meticulous about my chores, and never left any clothes there. In the OOBE, though, I didn't notice this.

I also didn't register the fact that the sofa in the OOBE had been our old, long-ago-discarded sofa. I didn't even question that, or the fact that there was a trench of dirt around it. In my living room! But in the OOBE I could feel the dirt in my hands. I *was* moving dirt. I sighed, I definitely need to become more aware in the OOB environment to recognize incongruities... if it is possible.

Six days later, I couldn't get to sleep. My mind kept racing for hours. When I got up in the morning I had only received four hours of sleep. I had to cancel driving on a field trip with my son's class. I didn't dare drive the distance we were to go and spend the whole day with the children on only four hours sleep. I was very angry, as I wanted to go with them and didn't want to break my promise that I would help, but, simultaneously, I didn't feel it would be safe.

After dropping Brian off at school, I lay down about 9:00 a.m. I thought to myself, "There had better be a darn good reason for me to miss that field trip."

Later I got out of bed, did chores around the house, and went out to our gray Caravan. After backing out of our driveway, I drove up the familiar, steep hill, then around the curving road beside the undeveloped canyon to my right. While doing so, the car suddenly went out of control, and I realized I was going to have a car accident.

The car went off the road, soaring into the canyon. Suspended above the canyon, I had time enough to think that I had better get out of the car before impact, and I immediately did. I *floated* out and over the car, and looked down at it from above. I could clearly see the desert shrubs and rocks, and the car falling into the canyon. When I realized I was OOB, quicker than thought, I was back in my body. It was ten o'clock.

I had done it again! It was so vivid! I was just sorry I had paid so little attention to what I had been doing in the house prior to going for the drive. Pleased at how little time it had taken me to get OOB, it appeared that extreme exhaustion aided the "getting out" process. Just prior to the OOBE, I had wondered if the reason I missed driving on the field trip was to avoid a car accident. I may have missed an accident on the trip, but I certainly didn't OOB.

Since my plans had changed for the day and I was still tired, I lay back down.

When I went downstairs later, my brother and Brian had just walked in the door of the house. I was pleasantly surprised, but asked how they could be here since Brian was supposed to be on his field trip. My brother shrugged his shoulders and indicated that they didn't know, they just were. So we enthusiastically hugged—I did love them both—but I knew I was OOB. This brother lived out of state.

I picked up some of Brian's homework paper and started writing what was happening (quite a habit from recording my dreams). When I looked to see what Brian and my brother were doing, they were beside the living room table, drawing with crayons and paper. Turning back to my note taking, I noticed what I had written wasn't on the paper!

Confused, I unjustifiably accused Brian of taking the paper on which I had been writing. When I looked at his paper, my notes weren't on there either. Then the phone rang and I answered it, still confused as to where my notes had disappeared. I talked to my younger sister for a few minutes, then set the phone down. It rang again, and someone else was on the line. It was the brother that was standing beside me!!

I was shocked. Words cannot describe the extent of my incomprehension. How could I be talking to him on the telephone when he was standing beside me? When I turned and asked him, he was as surprised as I was! Then someone else came on the line. It was another relative, an Aunt, and I could hear her as clearly as I had heard the others. My Aunt said, in a cheerful tone of voice, "Hi, I bet this is a surprise, talking to me." It was definitely her voice.

I was, by this time, quite bewildered. I set the

phone down and decided to go upstairs to see if I could see my body in bed. On the way, I became distracted by some newspapers on the floor. I didn't leave newspapers lying around. When I looked closer, the wallpaper near the papers looked similar to the wallpaper in my mother's house (where she kept a stack of old newspapers). When I reached the top of the stairs, I noticed the ceiling had water stains from a leak near the door to our bedroom. I told myself I would tell Bob about it so that we could have it repaired. Finally, I opened my eyes physically and came out of it.

What a shocking experience! And so utterly, undeniably real! As I thought about it, I felt it was meant to be disturbing so that I would consciously realize that I was OOB. It was such a long experience that I had difficulty recalling the exact sequence of events. I may have thought of Brian, so he materialized; but I hadn't thought of my brother or sister, and I *knew* I hadn't thought of the Aunt whose conversation I remembered. I rarely thought of her, since we were not that close, she lives far from me, and I heard news of her very infrequently.

I was slightly irritated at my difficulty remembering all that had happened. I couldn't remember the conversation I had had with my sister. I was in a dither wondering how my notes had vanished. As I thought about it, I recognized that it was probably completely understandable. The events were so real that I didn't pay attention to the detail as I would if I were visiting a new world. I seem to keep forgetting while OOB, that I am in the OOB environment. I always become involved with what is occurring around me, and need to be reminded where I am. I am sure the odd occurrences in the OOBEs were trying to do just that, wake me to a conscious realization of my non-physical circumstances. Evidently, the OOB environment is characteristic of the true human condition and its incomprehension of its "illusory" state. If we are multi-dimensional selves, which I was now almost positive was true, most of us certainly aren't aware of it.

One to two months later the house did have a leak at the exact spot specified in the OOBE. We had had a new air conditioner installed several months before this OOBE, and due to our infrequent desert rains, we were unaware it wasn't sealed properly after it was replaced. Along with everything else, the OOBE had been precognitive.

The next day I had another restless night and didn't fall asleep until 2:00 a.m. After returning home from taking Brian to school, I lay down about 8:35. I wondered how I could induce another OOBE (I never give up). Once I felt the swaying sensation, I remembered to imagine myself standing outside my body, and did; and was; and knew it.

I walked to the corner of the bedroom, determined to check out the atmosphere. I looked around and it seemed dim, not fully illuminated. As I turned to leave the bedroom, I thought I should look at my body. This was true courage on my part. I had seen it once before while fully out, and it had been quite a fright for me. Not that it was scary looking, but some portion of my soul rebelled at the idea I could be two places at once. I decided to be brave.

I turned around, faced the bed, and... it was gone! The bed, and my body in it, were gone. All I could see was brown carpet where the bed should have been. Strangely enough, I was mysteriously unconcerned. I rationalized that I was just blocking myself from seeing my body to avoid the stress on my psyche. That decided, I turned from that view and looked into an adjacent mirror. I could see myself in the mirror, and I looked perfectly natural. I had on the same clothes I was wearing physically - a turquoise top and blue jean shorts.

I started for the bedroom door and wondered what I would find downstairs. The slightest thought entered my mind, "Wouldn't it be funny if I walked out the door into a different place entirely?" As soon as I realized what I was doing, I clamped down on the thought. I evidently didn't do so soon enough. I walked out the door and turned to the right.

A young, blonde workman was kneeling on the floor beside a hole in the wall. He appeared to be fixing or working on the hole. Taken somewhat aback, I stopped beside him. I knew he was a thought form, or should have been. I thought I would try to will him away, but wondered if I would be able to. Of course, with that doubt in my mind, it didn't work. When I realized that, I demanded to know who he was.

I looked him straight in the eyes, ready to defend myself and my territory, if necessary. He shrank back at my ferocity, mumbled something like, he didn't know, he was just doing his job. He then got up, said he needed a tool, and walked down the stairs to the front door. I suspiciously watched him descend the stairs, and was simultaneously surprised.

This was no longer my home. It was some grand house being built, partially finished, with bare white walls near the door. The stairs were wide and curved downward. The front door was big with tall, thin windows on either side of it. The workman went out the door. I had followed him and locked the deadbolt behind him. I began looking around, when I noticed the workman come in to the right. I assumed there was another entrance there.

I didn't like the fact that the workman was still

there. I turned to watch him as he went to work on a ceiling fixture. He seemed innocent enough, so I decided, stranger or no stranger, I was OOB and I was going to explore. Since I didn't recognize the house, I asked if we were still in our city. When I didn't receive an answer, I looked out the window and could see desert shrubs. The room where I was standing was unfinished. I was disappointed that there was no furniture.

When I turned to look at the rest of the place, I saw rooms, many of them, with furniture. In one direction were the wide carpeted stairs we had just descended. To the right of the stairs were cabinets and shelves with decorative accessories on them. I noticed some sculptures: a pair of horses raised on their hind legs, facing each other. They were glass or porcelain with muted enameled colors. Then I turned around and walked up to a free-standing counter. On it were some real estate flyers. I picked one up and read the caption, Hueco Homes.

I looked further and saw more rooms with similar white/beige sofas in them. Could this have been a reflection in a mirror behind the sofa? It really looked too big to be a single-family home. It was a bright place, as if it received much daylight. Then suddenly, much to my chagrin, I felt this intense sexual urge. I was quite astonished, and irritated - what a time to have that happen!

I tried to ignore it, but it would not be dissuaded. I decided to take care of the situation, though I will not go into details. After a thoroughly pleasant experience, I returned to my body.

An interesting synchronicity, reality creation, happened concerning this OOBE. On August 13, 1992, as I was typing other OOB experiences into my computer database, I wondered about this one. I wondered if I would ever know if it was a real place I had visited, when the phone rang. On the telephone was a prerecorded message. I had just about hung up when I heard it was a real estate salesman calling to see if we were interested in some land development called Hueco Homes. I really wish there were Twilight Zone music accompanying events like this. This was the first time I had ever heard of any such development. I was used to these supposed "coincidences" appearing in my life, but this was a little much to shrug off.

Progress

If we really understand how dreams worked and allowed ourselves to explore dream levels, we'd see how the universe is formed. It is the... creative product, en masse, of our individual and joint dreams...our world is a dream level for some other types of consciousness; it's shared to some extent, then, and can serve as a meeting point.

Jane Roberts, The Unknown Reality, *Vol. 1, App. 11*

Quite pleased with my progress, I had the longest OOB to date on May 21, 1992. After totally relaxing, I had many visions, then I wished I could have one which would be an indication that it was now possible for me to be OOB. My wish was answered with a "vision" of an open window, and I knew I could leave my body. I rolled off the bed. A slight thought of concern for Brian crossed my mind, but I reminded myself he was fine, since he was at school. Evidently the correction of my initial thought didn't "take," for the next thing I knew I was following Brian and other children down the street outside our home.

A car pulling a trailer behind it stopped, and two men got out. They made the children stand in front of some rectangular units that looked like metal telephone junction boxes sticking out of the ground. I was watching and worried about the children. As I drew closer, I kept my eyes on my son as he moved around. The men finally left and the children were all right. With my concerns relieved, I immediately found myself back in bed.

Reflecting on the recent multi-dimensional events, I thought of Brian and how much I loved him, when I heard noises as if he were climbing the stairs. He walked into the room and jumped in bed with me. He was hugging me, as was his habit, and I hugged him back. I was aware of the intense affection and love we felt for each other, and the comfort and warmth of his hug. We expressed our love for each other, but I knew it couldn't actually be Brian, since, physically, he was in school. I decided to try to make him disappear. If he was a thought-form, then he should disappear. My conscience bothered me for even thinking of such a thing. I lay there feeling guilty for having such a thought. Evidently, to make someone--even a thought-form of someone you love-- disappear isn't easy. So he didn't, but mentally I still wanted him to leave so I could continue my OOBE.

Some thought must have taken, for Brian then got up and walked across the room. As he did so, I noticed he didn't look like himself anymore. He looked misshapen with wide shoulders, a short body, long neck, and a bald head. I think that when I had thought it couldn't be Brian in my arms and wondered if it was some kind of monster I was holding, the thought-form turned into one. The swiftness of thought and the instant materialization in the OOB environment can be quite challenging at times. I was then aware of only myself lying in bed.

I was hearing noises though. A radio was on very loud, and I heard people talking. Then, since I knew I was in the OOB environment, I thought about where I would want to go if I could go anywhere at all. After living in the desert for almost twenty years, and due to my love of the ocean, the first thought to enter my mind was water. The next thing I knew I was off. Flying through the air like a jet plane. This was the most heavenly experience possible. I could feel the air rushing past me. This was fantastically refreshing! I even tried moving my arms and legs, mid-flight, to see what it felt like. I wasn't disappointed. It was wonderful. Only seconds, maybe thirty, seemed to have passed before I found myself over water.

I was looking down at the waves rocking in the sunlight and at what looked like tiny brown boats. I must have thought they looked like toys, for the next thing I knew, I heard children's voices at play. I entered the water and had another delightful sensation. I was definitely in water. It felt like water. But I wasn't getting wet! I enjoyed that and luxuriated in the sensation of small waves lapping my body for a while.

Soon, when the novel experience ceased to fascinate me, I began to wonder where I was. I hadn't aimed for any specific location, just water. I began observing the water more closely. The water was brownish and didn't look like any ocean water I had seen before. I wondered if I was in a sewer. With that thought, I saw a round, metal object under the water. The children near me made some comments about taking it home to show their parents. As I doubted where I was, I started thinking again. I didn't know where I was, but I knew I wanted to be at the ocean. So I thought of the ocean and sand under my feet, and immediately transferred to another location and felt millions of granules of stardust under my toes. It felt magnificent.

Suddenly, I was back in my bed again, but I didn't want to quit. I was having the time of my life and wanted more. Straining upward, I forgot to think my way out. I was having trouble vacating my body again. When I heard a distinct male voice say, "Stand on your feet," I remembered the correct procedure. I imagined myself standing on my feet, and I was out. The voice spoke again and told me to go out on the balcony and wait. So I walked over to the balcony.

Then I wondered who was talking to me, as I hadn't thought of anything to cause a thought-form to manifest. Without turning my head, I could somehow see behind me, through my head, and saw two long-robed figures! One was tall in dark robes, and the other was shorter in light robes. Unfortunately, at that moment, I became distracted by another sound.

There was a slight breeze blowing through the cottonwoods beside our balcony. I knew it was not a hard wind, but it sounded quite loud rustling through the leaves. The thought went through my mind that it sounded like a gale. The next thing I knew, I was down on the street below me, fighting my way through what felt like a tornado! It was extremely windy, and I had to really force myself up the street, about one hundred feet, to my back door.

What a situation, and still my mind did not stop! As I was struggling to reach the back door with the wind blowing in my face trying to force me downhill, I wondered what our backyard would look like in the future. I saw what appeared to be a massive fort along our back fence - like a child's fort. I thought, that can't be. Anyone who would buy our house probably wouldn't have many children, and I didn't think we would build anything like that. Then I saw the backyard enclosed in a five to six-foot-high fence. That made more sense to me, especially if they built houses in the canyon across the street from us.

As I approached the door near the carport, I wondered what I would find in the house. I thought wouldn't it be neat if I saw the proverbial White Light that people have been known to encounter in Near Death Experiences. I opened the door of the house and walked into white light. I closed the door behind me. I tentatively walked toward the living room. I could hear what sounded like water dripping in the house, and sounds of a storm came from outside (residue from my gale, no doubt). I couldn't make out any form, nor did I feel any intense love or any other sensation from the light. It was kind of eerie and must have concerned me, for I again found myself back in my body.

I still didn't want to stop, though, but had trouble vacating my body. I kept trying to lift out, when I needed to think myself out. While lying there I wondered what my future held, and "saw" a man walking toward a car. It looked like it was covered in brown suede, and was parked in a big, underground parking garage. The man had dark hair, was approximately 5'9" tall, and was dressed in a long-sleeved shirt and pants. I thought I heard a voice say, "This is your destiny." What that meant, I didn't know. Was it someone I would meet in the future, or just more thought-forms? Then I was aware of being in bed again and of hearing the telephone ring physically. I thought I had better answer it. So I struggled to awareness, and I mean struggled, and answered the phone.

After dealing with the physical telephone call, I reviewed all that had occurred OOB. At the beginning of this experience, when I was thinking that I didn't have to worry about Brian then was immediately doing so - does this indicate that negatives don't register in the OOB environment? Brian did end up being unharmed in the incident, so possibly it was just a manifestation of the whole thought process. I don't know.

Not long after this OOB, we went out of town and visited the Gulf of Mexico for the first time. The water looked exactly like that in my recent OOB. There were several tall buoys, or something similar in the distance there, but not exactly like those I had witnessed in the OOB. I was seeing them from ground level, however, not from the air. The man in my destiny view looked surprisingly similar to my son's soccer coach in the fall. He even had a car like the one I had seen in the OOBE. I didn't meet him until sometime in August or September.

Interaction

A practitioner of this ancient art learns first of all how to become conscious in <u>normal</u> terms, while in the sleep state...All of this, however, is but a beginning for our dream-art scientist, for he or she then begins to recognize the fact of involvement with many different levels and <u>kinds</u> of reality and activity.

Seth, The Unknown Reality, *Vol. 1, Session 700*

In August I had several more OOBEs, one of which began in the state of anger. I was very angry at my recent lack of OOBEs and became determined, angry or not, to get out. It worked, but it left me wondering about the connection. Did the amount of energy generated by my aggressive feelings facilitate the OOBE, or was it just my intense desire? I had been OOB many times before without being angry, but there were several occasions when dogged determination was definitely a factor. If that were true, since I don't like being angry, I decided to return to a technique I had used previously.

Before sleep I told myself I would come awake in the most significant dream of the night. As it turned out, I never felt I slept all night. I was experiencing events, but I thought it was all real physically. This night I was lying in bed and thought I heard someone outside on our deck. Any kind of sound seems to be a prime focusing factor in my OOBEs. The thought that the sounds might be caused by a burglar crossed my mind. I didn't hear any further noise, so I relaxed and let my mind wander. I started thinking of how terrible it would be if some stranger were in the house. The next thing I knew...

Someone grabbed my arm and attacked me. Though the figure was strong and keeping me pinned by my forearms, I fought back with my legs. Kicking and wiggling, we struggled in silence. I didn't want to scream. I didn't want to awaken my son and scare him. What a fright! I was struggling with this person for what seemed to me like too long a period, but it was probably only minutes. I couldn't figure out why Bob, who was lying beside us, wasn't waking. When we rolled over him as he slept, I realized that this couldn't be real. I must be fighting a thought-form, and I came out of it.

Totally exasperated, I was quite upset with myself. Where do these thoughts come from? They may seem like normal, healthy thoughts to the average person, but in the OOB state I can't afford to have thoughts like these. Any fears, doubts, or beliefs in evil will manifest there if I think of them. When would that ever sink in? When would I know and live that? I really needed to clean up my mind and remember that life is good. I am always perfectly safe and experience only what I believe to be true. Sighing, I thought I needed to remind myself as well that not only would I come awake in my dreams, but that I would realize I was dreaming!

The next time I went out, it was from the middle of a dream. After much prior vivid dream activity...

I was hovering near my son's school. I decided I should return home. Immediately, I was outside my home - but not my current home. I was at the doorstep of my childhood home! I noticed snow piled up beside the door, and I used a key to enter. Walking in, I was surprised to see a brilliant white light at the other end of the room. As my eyes adjusted to the light, I saw the house was devoid of furniture, something I had never seen before. Puzzled by these strange circumstances, I saw my mother there, looking much younger than her current age, and I consciously realized I must be OOB. Once that happened, I was immediately back in my physical body still aware of the OOB environment, but now my mother was superimposed on the background of my OOB/physical bedroom. She was still moving around, talking on the end of a long telephone cord we had once had, but she was now in my bedroom.

My mother disappeared when I told myself she couldn't actually be there. I began trying to leave my body, of which I was now conscious, and was becoming quite frustrated. I thought, "If only I could be put squarely on the carpet, then I would be okay and able to function." The strangest thing happened. I felt "someone" lift my legs straight in the air as if they were a rectangle of wood. They did the same thing with the upper part of my body as well, as if it, too, were a piece of wood. Then I was placed upright on the carpet beside the bed. What was funny was, I felt square! That is, my normally shapely body felt cuboid, with sharp, angular edges. Very unusual. Sometimes your thoughts in that environment can definitely cause you to experience strange sensations, but they did get me OOB.

A few days before lying down for this rest period, I had decided to try an experiment. If I did succeed in reaching the OOB environment, I wanted to see if I could read something physical from that state. To that end, I often opened a book at random and left it on a bedside table. This day I had done so, as well.

After my unconventional but effective entrance into the OOB environment, I walked over to the table and looked at the open book. I tried to focus, but nothing seemed to register. Then all of a sudden, I was seeing pictures in a comic book called *The*

Phantom. I was turning pages and looking at a character in a purple hood and tights, and reading some of the brightly colored captions. I don't remember what I read, but I couldn't understand why I was perusing a comic book.

I was then distracted by a black-and-white cat sitting in the chair beside the table the book was on. I started petting the cat, running my fingers through its soft fur. I became concerned about the time and checked the clock radio. There was one on my side of the bed which said 3:05 p.m. I realized there wasn't one on my side physically, so I looked to the left at the one that was supposed to be there physically. The physical one seemed to say the same time, so I checked my watch and it was the same time, too. I panicked and literally dove for my body. I would be late picking Brian up from school.

After shaking myself into my body, I discovered it was only 1:40. I wasn't sure why this happened. Possibly to return me to my body so I would remember all the details of what I had experienced. Of course, I then remembered that I always set an alarm clock before I lie down so I won't be concerned about being out too long.

Upon recording the events of the OOBE in my notebook, I checked to where the book I was trying to read had been opened. The first line of the page read, and I quote, "'The Phantom's Revenge,' he grinned at me. 'I made it with plaster.'" This was totally unexpected. My mouth dropped open in surprise, then transformed into a smile of delight. I had forgotten that anything like this was even in the book! Evidently I *did* read the line, and in the OOB atmosphere, it was immediately transformed into images I could recognize!

Since I am not very familiar with comic books, several days later I visited a local comic book collector's store to see if they had any book by that name. Much to my surprise and delight, they did, and the main character, the Phantom, was dressed in a purple-hooded, tight outfit, just as I had seen him in my OOBE.

Past Associations

*Some dead friends and relatives do visit you,
projecting from their own level of reality into yours, but
you cannot as a rule perceive their forms. They are not
more ghostly, or "dead," however, than you are when
you project into their reality - as you do, from the sleep
state.*

Seth, Seth Speaks, *Session 540*

November 1992. A couple of weeks before
we went on vacation to California, I
decided I wanted to add some gemstones
to some old rings I had. I opened my jewelry box and
took out the rings to determine if any still fit my
aging fingers. I picked up the wedding band my first
husband had given me. As I was trying to put it on
my pinkie finger, I felt a force trying to put it on my
wedding-band finger! I couldn't figure out what was
going on. I thought to myself, "I don't want it on that
finger. I won't be wearing it there." Mystified, I then
exerted force of my own to put it on my pinkie finger.
I decided it was unsuitable, in any case, and found a
couple of other rings that would work rather nicely.

After this experience, though, Tim was on my
mind. Our failed marriage came to mind. How it was
unfortunate that the marriage hadn't worked out.
How, if parallel realities existed, it did work out in
another reality. I felt love for him and knew that he
had loved me, even though we could not live
together. Though saddened by these thoughts, I

knew I was also much happier in my present circumstances. I knew life always had a purpose, and for some reason, we were only to be together for the time we had been. I hoped he was okay and wished him well. I sent him love and forgiveness for all the pain we caused each other.

Thoughts of him kept surfacing for several minutes. I had no desire to see him or know what was happening in his life. I couldn't figure out why he kept coming to mind. He did, for some unknown reason, and I eventually had to forcefully expel the thoughts from my mind. They were so persistent. I hadn't seen nor heard of Tim in several years. I knew he had remarried and where he had lived a couple of years ago, but that was all.

During the next few days, I was busy planning our trip. One of the friends we were to visit called to see when we would be arriving; she told me she had called the operator from work and asked for my phone number, only she asked for my name as it was when I was married to my first husband. We laughed and talked about senility.

While on vacation visiting with family and friends, one night after dinner as we were sitting around the table the strangest impulse entered my mind. I had the inclination to ask my cousin if she knew whether a former husband of hers was still alive! I couldn't believe it! Shocked at the thought, I didn't ask the question. How rude; even though, I had to admit, I would want to know if Tim had died. It would be awful not knowing. I shook my head at these strange thoughts and assured myself that I would know.

The next morning my cousin came bounding out of her bedroom quite astonished. Her radio had just come on of its own accord. She was certain she hadn't set the alarm, and even if she accidentally had, it went off at a time for which it was never set!

She was beside herself, excited over the strange occurrence. She decided our dead grandmother was telling her to get up since she had company. For some unknown reason, though I didn't say so, I knew the message was for me. I became uneasy.

Later that day when my cousin called her boyfriend who was dying of cancer, he said the night before he, too, had had a strange thing happen. He was an antique collector, and somehow a music box that hadn't worked in years started playing without being touched by human hands. Both were perplexed by the strange proceedings. I became increasingly uneasy. We continued with our fun and had a wonderful visit, but during our long drive home I could feel myself becoming more and more tense.

When we got home, I discovered the reason for all of the unusual phenomena. In the mail was a letter from a friend informing me that my first husband, the musician, had died of cancer several weeks before. Does life exist after death and can that consciousness influence reality? I have no doubt that it does.

Hot Stuff

Let me take this moment to state again that there are no devils or demons, except as you create them out of your belief. As mentioned earlier, good and evil effects are basically illusions. In your terms all acts, regardless of their seeming nature, <u>are</u> part of a greater good. I am not saying a good end justifies what you would consider an evil action. While you still accept the effects of good and evil, then you had better choose the good.

Seth, Seth Speaks, *Session 587*

One morning I was feeling extremely drowsy, so I returned to bed at 9:05 a.m. I told myself I would come awake in my dreams and realize I was dreaming. The phone rang and I answered it. It was a strange call. Someone, using what sounded like a phony Southern accent, asked if this were a business or residence. I told her residence and she hung up.

Puzzled, I returned to my relaxing and thought about OOBEs and that it would be interesting to have one in a different setting. Then I fell asleep, and in my "dream" the phone rang and I answered it.

I couldn't understand what the caller was saying, though it seemed to be about coaching soccer (I was the registrar for a local youth soccer league). There were many pauses and garbled speech. I decided I must be OOB, so I got up and walked by the bureau where I'd left a book open. I am not sure whether I looked at it or not, but I know I continued downstairs.

I was in unfamiliar surroundings. The bedroom door was massive, much bigger than ours and, in contrast to our white one, was made out of a dark wood. It opened opposite of its physical counterpart. A few inconsequential things happened before I walked by several rooms with many book shelves in them. One shelf was similar to a store display unit with many copies of a red book on it. My son walked up and showed me a book. I knew it couldn't be Brian, but this time, I decided to just let the events unfold to see what would happen.

I took the book from Brian as we were walking down the hall. We entered another room filled with colorful books. I thought they might be children's books, they looked so bright and cheerful. I glanced at the binding of one which had LuLu printed on it. The only connection I could make was that there was once a comic book character by that name. I was trying to recall which comic book it was; the one about the little red demon came to mind, when Brian asked me what the title was of the book I was holding.

I looked at the book, and its title was *Get Awake While You Can*. What a strange title, I thought. I looked closer at the cover, and underneath the title was what appeared to be an intricate drawing of the human brain. As I tried to focus I thought, it almost looks like a psychological ink blot test. As I stared at it, it took on, to me, the shape of a devil's face. Startled, I immediately set the book down, a frown on my face, and we walked into another room.

In there, a dark-haired child was seated cross-legged on the floor looking at a pile of comic books. Walking beside him was a devil in yellow pants and shirt! The devil had an arrow-tipped tail, black hair, and was carrying a pitchfork. I stopped in consternation and thought, "That is ridiculous. There are no such things as devils. He looks like a caricature." With that comment, the devil disappeared. I glanced over the child's shoulder to see what he was reading. It was a copy of the comic book *Hot Stuff*, about the little red demon.

Many more insignificant things happened before I eventually joined a group of unfamiliar people in a foyer. They were standing around in groups as if at a cocktail party. This was a particularly long OOB, and I could feel myself tiring and beginning to drift mentally. I noticed myself observing what was happening but not taking it in. Then I heard someone say, "She's not concentrating." I was too exhausted to analyze the situation, to find out who these people were, or who had made the comments. I turned, ascended the stairs and re-animated my body.

Once back in the physical, I thought of the OOBE. It was not dreamlike. I had walked, talked, hugged, but the subject matter was strange. I decided that it was probably caused by the strange telephone call I received just before relaxing. Strangeness was on my mind. As I got up to leave the room, I glanced at the book I had left open on the bureau. The book had been randomly opened to the following passage:

Be Afraid of nothing

you have within you -

all wisdom

all power

all strength

all understanding.

Eileen Caddy
The Dawn of Change

Conclusion

All That Is is alive within the least of Itself, aware within, for example, the molecule. It endows all of Its parts - or Its creations - with Its own abilities that then act as inspiration, impetus, guiding lines and principles, by which these parts then seek to further create themselves, their own worlds and systems. This is freely given.

Seth, Seth Speaks, *Session 580*

A good friend once commented to me that we are so confident we can overcome anything when we enter physical reality, that many of us choose to experience traumatic events simply because we are so positive we can handle those experiences. Some of us are simply adventurers at heart. Given the nature of my experiences both in and out of body, I would venture that I am one of those thrill seekers.

I would like to say that I know everything there is to know about OOBEs, but I cannot. I would like to say that all there is to know about OOBEs is known, but I cannot. I would like to say that what you experience OOB will be completely relevant, self-explanatory, intelligible, and non-bizarre from a physical perspective, but again, I cannot. The experiences are so varied, personal and enigmatic that much research is still needed in the OOB field to help clarify this aspect of reality.

I wrote this book as I did in order to give my audience a glimpse of what it was like experiencing spontaneous OOBEs. My life, as I mentioned, was a busy one. When my OOBEs began in earnest, I would have my experience and write it down; if any connection to my physical life was readily apparent, I would note it. After many years of experience with this aspect of reality I have been able to reach some conclusions which I will now share with you. Beginning with the first chapter, I will comment on each chapter.

The Visitor

We cannot divorce our physical experiences from our metaphysical ones. All experiences, physical or not, are tied to our psychological stance in the world. My conscious entrance into the OOB aspect of reality began with the appearance of the Indian Brave. At the time I was experiencing a deep sense of security, happiness and relaxation after an active period of anxiety and tension involving my new marital situation. This sense of contentment is a necessary component to any sustained out-of-body investigations. If you do not trust yourself and your Source, it is exceedingly difficult to travel out of body.

New Memory

Much of society would assume that my new memory of the Frontier Party was what is now commonly referred to as a blocked memory come to light. This is a valid hypothesis, but when psychologists speak of blocked memories they usually refer to memories of a traumatic nature. My new memory could not truthfully be considered such an event. I was delighted by the Frontier Party and had no real reason to hide it from my conscious mind. Another explanation of this event encompasses the possibility that if we live in a mutable world, a world in which past and future experiences can be freely chosen out of myriad probabilities, this new memory could well have been a new experience inserted into this probable world by my Higher Self to enhance the likelihood that I would study the nature of consciousness. The Indian Brave had been a significant incentive for such research, but the memory of enjoying myself as a child, freely and uninhibitedly playing with states of consciousness, aspects of mind and focuses of the soul, was much more of an incentive.

Prediction

Psychic, intuitive knowledge is available to all who choose to acknowledge and use it. My astrological chart, while interesting, does not define who I am. I choose who I will be by the choices I make in my attitudes, beliefs and intentions. Hal's prediction of my first marriage's demise was due solely to his belief in the chart, his psychic abilities and my unconscious decision to encounter those predictions in physical form.

The astrological reading, however accurate, was an unconsciously chosen event mirroring my fears and judgmental attitudes toward my new marriage. The reading was another triggering mechanism, as Hal's predictions *did* entice me to learn more about man's spiritual nature and the nature of time and reality.

Symptoms

At the time I was experiencing the phenomena, I didn't realize the true significance of my "psychic fingers." My unconscious body, which is entirely conscious on a multi-dimensional level, knew and found the cards and locations I needed. In fact, I would venture the cells of the cards and spaces easily, effortlessly and accurately responded to my desire to find them. At one time, I would have refuted this evidence of the cooperative nature of life. I no longer do so. I believe the physical world is as responsive as the OOB world. Once accepted as a valid hypothesis of world construction, evidence of the cooperative nature of life abounds. Like huge magnets our desires and beliefs attract responses from the life around us. It is a cooperative world, if we only allow it to be.

The Omega and the Alpha

My interlude with Tim, my first husband, was interesting now that I can look back on it with some perspective. While a teenager I frequently imagined how romantic it would be to be married to a Rock-and-Roll musician. I was a big Beatles fan, and thought it would be the most fun lifestyle possible. The desire to experience that type of lifestyle was fulfilled, but my conflicting beliefs about what constituted a normal marriage were not met in that union. These conflicting beliefs and our negatively judgmental attitudes toward each other finally led to the downfall of the marriage.

I firmly believe that if I had accepted my responsibility for consciously creating my reality through my thoughts and beliefs and changed my beliefs to more constructive ones, I would have remained married to Tim. That is, through the literal reality-creating mechanism of positive beliefs we would have moved into the probable reality where we had a successful marriage.

The appearance in my life of my present husband

was the direct result of my intense, emotion-laden visualizing just prior to meeting him. A Christian friend once commented that I wasn't giving credit where the credit was due implying that God, using traditional definitions, had answered my prayer. But I am giving credit where credit is due. All That Is, God, if you will, exists and functions in all that is. That means in you, me, the floor, a crocus, and an ant. Consciousness - God - and the ability to create permeates all reality. We are not separate. "He" is us, though, of course, much more than us. We share "His" abilities to manifest reality and co-create our reality through our intense desires, beliefs and thoughts. Meeting Bob was one very obvious instance in which I created my reality. In fact when Bob and I met, this was a joint creation of ours - as all interactions are. Bob was as ready for a meaningful relationship as I was. Our joint desires merged and found fulfillment in each other.

Discovery

The photograph of White Plume, the American Indian brave, and its appearance in my life was and still is an enigmatic experience for me. Was I White Plume? Am I White Plume in a simultaneous, multi-dimensional aspect of being? I still don't know, but there is one metaphysical fact I do know concerning this event. A piece of my life, a future event, visited my conscious mind at least nine years before I encountered it physically. If I had chosen another probable reality where I never met my second husband, the Brave would have been just another ghostly visitation, or possibly would not have been experienced. It appears to me that a future self, a me that knew I was to marry my second husband, sent me the Indian Brave as a sign. Though I didn't realize it at the time, it was a message of a better tomorrow.

The Straw

Given that thoughts manifest themselves OOB, one could naturally assume the Indian Chief was an immediate thought manifestation. While this could be entirely true, the spontaneous nature of the experience and the multi-dimensional nature of our being implies another explanation. I do not recall premeditatively choosing to be born in North Dakota, to marry a man and move with him to New Mexico, to divorce him and marry another man whose first wife wrote a book about her American Indian Great-Grandfather. From a Higher Self perspective this was all a rather marvelous creation of woven significances, probabilities, if you will, to create these "coincidences" in my life. The "coincidences" appear even more significant when considering the fact I had no conscious interest in American Indian affairs.

Every event in our lives has personal significance, however. We are given clues through our daily impulses, thoughts, and dreams to aspects, i.e., other incarnations, of our grander multi-personhood selves. I believe I was actually sharing the experience of another life lived as an American Indian. The event was too alive, vital and totally unexpected to be other than what it seemed to be.

Paradox

The unseen guest who visited my son and me has many possible explanations concerning the origin of its existence. It could have been a ghost. It could have been a god. It could have been many things, but considering my OOBEs, I believe from a multi-dimensional, simultaneous time perspective it may have been a future me that came to our home. The reason I say this is not only because of my personal encounters with future events and people, but a friend of mine, Sandra Stevens, author of *Being Alive is Being Psychic* and *Relating Psychically: Psychic Influences on Relationships*, once had a client go out of body during a past life regression session. Sandra could sense his OOB body as it traveled past her. This may have been what my son and I felt as well. I particularly relate to when Brian was a baby and often think fondly back to that time. If I were to consciously visit a past self, I would choose that time, and I believe Brian would recognize and respond to the love I feel for him.

Memories

Evidence of life after death has existed since time immemorial. It exists today. Whatever belief structure currently reigns influences what shape after-life forms will take and in what actions they will engage. A fascinating study, *Appearances of the Dead: A Cultural History of Ghosts* by R. C. Finucane, documented how ghostly sightings throughout history clearly reflected the beliefs of the citizens alive at that time. The information given by the "ghosts" was valid, but their images and behavior always mirrored what man believed to be true regarding the after-death state.

I find this fascinating and in complete agreement with my OOBEs. Having been conscious OOB, I know the I-ness of me exists apart from my body. Near-death experiences also verify that we do indeed exist in some form after death. Maybe Ben did see Christ and Del did see her mother, both of which were representations, forms, taken on by consciousness.

Dream Life

For beings who are scientifically considered accidents of nature, our consciousness, creativity, dreams and out-of-body experiences belie this attitude. If studied and recalled, dreams and projections of consciousness provide energy, inspiration, answers to problems, and glimpses into past and future events. We can no longer assume dreams are illusory when aspects of those dreams become physical fact. It appears to me dreams are corridors to current and adjacent realities in time and space. We merely need to learn the rules of passage to these locations.

The Gift

Since I do believe we create our own reality, my cancer was a wake-up call for me. It reminded me that I am responsible for my life, the shape it takes and how I will live it. Nor do we live alone. Each of us interacts with other human beings and agrees to experience joint creations. Though my cancer turned out to be minor, it served several purposes. It pointed out my need to become consciously aware of erroneous beliefs. It also reassured my husband: he was given the evidence that one can have cancer and recover from it. It rekindled his faith in the life process and affirmed our belief that no one dies unless he/she is ready to do so on some level. Death and illness serve psychological purposes despite the grief they engender.

Awakening

The precognitive dreams which followed my cancer were tremendous psychological aides for me. They cheered me up immensely and gave me incentive not to give up hope. They demonstrated that even as I was apparently messing up my life, I was never alone. My Higher Self was helping me and was there for me if I would only open my eyes to the goodness and better probabilities that surrounded me. These dreams showed me I possessed abilities of which I was unaware but would prove quite enlightening if pursued.

Soul Sight

There were several factors which led to the activation of my Soul Sight. Shortly after I accepted the fact that no matter what evidence was before my eyes — cancer, death, mayhem — life was good; my Source and I could be trusted; my Soul Sight was activated. Prior to this fundamental realization, for approximately one year I concentrated as much as possible in the present. Thoughts were noticed and released from my awareness, but what I was seeing, sensing, feeling, smelling in my immediate environment was what I concentrated on. Wandering, idle daydreaming was not allowed. This trust and focusing were direct forerunners to the onset of my Soul Sight experiences.

Flight

My shape-shifting experience as a bird was rather intriguing. Shamans have been engaging in this activity for centuries, of course, but as with most metaphysical issues, they have not been given credence by mainstream Western society. Seth, in *The Individual and The Nature of Mass Events* by Jane Roberts, made these comments in Session 838: "There is no such thing as a cat consciousness, basically speaking, or a bird consciousness. In those terms, there are instead simply consciousnesses that choose to take certain focuses... Then there is no prepackaged, predestined particular consciousness that is meant to be human, either." In the next Session he went on to say that he was not referring to the Eastern belief in transmigration of animal souls into human form. He was saying quite simply that consciousness pervades all known space, and we choose what it is we wish to experience. Consciousness is volatile enough to merge, combine with, or create whatever it wishes to experience be that plant, animal or molecule.

Given this mutability of consciousness, did I suddenly appear as a bird gliding over an ocean in this world or another? Did I magically appear out of nothingness to enjoy the southern ocean breezes? Is our world composed of our own materializations which we form in our desire to have company in our physical journey? And do we do this constantly with no memory of our role in its creation? If we try, can we recall our participation in these manifestations?

This is not just idle speculation. According to Quantum Mechanics and David Bohm's Quantum Potential Theory as described in his book, *Wholeness and the Implicate Order*, science is catching up with metaphysical knowledge. Since the description of this theory is beyond the scope of this book, I will let the reader verify it for himself. I will say, however, scientific theory now corroborates that we literally create our own realities.

A Voice in the Night

Not only do we choose to experience our lives, but when we ask for answers to life's questions, we receive them. The OOBE must be studied carefully. I have noticed incidences in the OOB state wherein not only was I experiencing interesting situations, but later details in those situations were definitely future events. Definite precognition. Sometimes the events are quite mundane and insignificant, but still precognitive.

One time all I saw were a pair of hands holding a butterfly. Several days later, my husband did just that as he was rescuing butterflies that willingly sat on his hand while he moved them from their imprisonment on an out-of-state friend's partially glassed-in porch. Neither of us had any foreknowledge that he would be engaging in this kind of activity.

So why do we receive information of insignificant future events? Shouldn't I be receiving the formula for nuclear fission or recipes to eradicate world hunger? I believe the reason is quite simply that those are not my predominant interests. If they were, I would receive insight into solutions to those problems. Our desires are met. My desire when I began my quest was simply to learn of consciousness and its abilities. I am succeeding in that goal.

Dimensions

Our consciousness is capable of so many heretofore unexamined phenomena. When my Soul Sight was activated, I was thrilled beyond measure, and yet the events were so varied as to make them seem almost incomprehensible. I persisted merely because I knew there had to be logic and I wanted to understand. When thoughts expanded and eagerly took form in this responsive environment, I had to train myself to be aware of my thoughts on a constant basis.

I knew symbols could be involved in the use of my Soul Sight as well as bona fide persons, places and things. Many instances were what is commonly referred to as Remote Viewing episodes where you are "seeing" valid objects but are not aware of a spiritual counterpart to the body. You are merely a point of consciousness viewing aspects of physical reality. Since I was initially unaware of the truth of thought manifestation during the use of Soul Sight, I have no way now of determining which were remote-viewing episodes and which were thought-form manifestations.

Another concept Seth introduced was that other portions of ourselves could be interacting with someone else while we were physically active. My interacting with my son and husband could very well have been true interaction. I have yet to interact OOB with a known physical person who is also conscious of being OOB. I do however believe it is entirely possible and know people who have done so.

Future Events

Time and space travel OOB and in our dreams is possible. Throughout this book I use the conventionally accepted terms such as precognition, precognitive dreams, and future events to describe such travel. I find these terms misleading, however. We have the capability to travel through space and time now. No spaceships or time machines are necessary for such travel - only our in-born consciousness.

Space travel was evident when I "met" my former husband and his new wife and when I "visited" my sister in the Philippines. Time travel was demonstrated by the visit with the baby prior to the baby shower and by the drive to the closed freeway entrance. All instances of time and space travel had a definite personal emotional significance for me. This may be a key to further investigations.

Getting Out

The inner body, the shape our consciousness can take, varies tremendously. At this point I would venture we may take any form while OOB and still maintain an awareness of ourselves as ourselves. Transfer into a form or shape is immediate once awareness of the physical is subdued.

My experience of floating out of body and seeing the heretofore unknown physical condominiums assured me that I was definitely OOB and not merely experiencing mental constructs. When I projected consciously and faced myself, I learned it is less stressful on the psyche to project from the dream state. When projecting from the dream state, the psyche is in its familiar sleep state, and no trauma is associated with projecting from there.

Loving

My loving experience in which I maintained an awareness of the godliness of all life taught me that love and total concentration enable us to be aware of the spiritual environment in which our physicality is couched. Not only does love help create the most pleasant reality possible, but by maintaining a state of love we demonstrate that we are definitely more than our physical bodies while we are totally conscious. We have access to our Higher Selves, our souls, at all times. There are no goals to reach. No programs to follow. No souls to redeem. If we can maintain the state of love and gratitude, we can become aware of our true nature now.

Our bodies do continue to function normally while OOB from the awake state. We still breathe, our blood still pumps, our cells still divide and multiply; but I am uncertain as to the amount of activity our bodies can sustain. Sitting in the chair took little effort. Walking further across the room may have been impossible. But human consciousness is mobile and independent of brain activity! This goes against what we have been taught for decades, but it doesn't make the fact any less true.

Energy Transfers

Energy comes in all forms. Dream images are often not only images, but conduits for energy and knowledge. For years after experiencing some of my dreams, I would be physically reenergized just by reading or recalling them. The energy was so intense that at times I didn't think I would ever be able to get some of these dreams in typed format; I frequently had to stand and release the energy I was feeling.

In the first dream of this chapter where I was engaging in some sort of higher learning at the "college," did the two girls who were frozen into statues symbolically signify two aspects of myself which I chose not to manifest in physical form? Or were they two aspects of my personality, or beliefs, which I was dispensing with? I know at this time in my life I was coming to terms with the commonly held belief that one needs to change in order to progress spiritually. I have since learned that is not the case.

I do not believe all dreams are symbolic, however. There must be ways to differentiate which dream images are symbolic and which are not. I haven't yet discovered the rules, but I continue to try. As far as the butterfly/angel dream is concerned, while I do not believe in the existence of angels per se, I do believe in various types of consciousness. There are millions of planets about which we know little. There are consciousnesses in nature we don't recognize or acknowledge. This dream could well have been my representation of and interaction with a Butterfly Consciousness. Physical size and shape do not necessarily define the size and shape of consciousness, as my own OOB excursions have demonstrated.

My Wild Woman dream occurred long before I knew that the Wild Woman was considered an archetypal form and before a popular book regarding the subject matter was in print. Some concepts evidently have more power associated with them. When you think of the energy behind religious myths and how religions have transformed civilizations, it is readily apparent that some dreams and ideas contain more energy than others. It may be that man imbues these objects with his own energy, thus making them, en masse, more powerful constructs to encounter.

The informative part of the Wild Woman dream for me was that focus and color are conduits to other levels of OOB, dream, or soul realities. My concentration in the dream on the colored dots, which signified different times, transported me into another time period and location. Further research is needed to determine exactly which color will take me where and when.

Lucidity

Several times I have had too brief encounters with Beings of Light. At this time, I don't know if I saw their natural state, their aura, the unsheathed form consciousness takes when not attached to physical shapes, or just energy in its natural state. In any case, it is always awe-inspiring and energizing to encounter Beings of Light.

Please notice the dream where I encountered the swooping birds and consider them a possible symbolic interpretation of fun-filled free flight. Notice the symbology of being elevated to higher floors. Do we not have the words to describe exuberant free-from-form states of being or relatively higher, more advanced dimensions, but instead use physical images to express the indescribable feelings and experiences? I often believe this is more true than not in waking reality as well as in dreams and OOBEs.

When I visited my deceased relatives, initially I was in a protective enclosure. I don't believe anything could have harmed me, but possibly my ignorance of how to function in that reality was being shielded so I could visit there. The symbology of the enclosure may also have been a creation of my unconscious mind to make my conscious mind more relaxed while doing the unthinkable - visiting the dead. The fact that a still living Aunt and cousin were there intrigues me. Were they visiting the dead as well as I, only unconsciously?

Dream Lucidity was always the result of concentration in whatever environment I happened to be, whether that concentration was due to beauty, intellectual curiosity or the hope that I was meeting with someone I loved. I use the term dream lucidity merely because it is a well-known phrase. I view all instances of lucidity, remote viewing, visions, false awakenings, or OOBEs as projections of consciousness. None is more important than the next, though some projections have longer durations than others.

Frequently I have found that when some event has me confused, it is an indication that I am probably OOB. Rarely am I confused physically, but frequently I am when OOB.

False Awakening

In my false-awakening dreams I was learning to maintain a conscious recognition of the space I was occupying. At one point I would be in my home, but often when I walked through a doorway, I would be in a new location. There may be some currently unknown directional movement or invisible portal which acts as a location transfer point. More research should clarify this aspect of OOB experiences.

The stranger who was fixing tiles in one false-awakening dream may have been a "helper" of some sort. A consciousness there to assist me if such aid were necessary. The two broken tiles could have been representations of Brian and me broken out of our physical forms. In this particular OOBE, why my childhood friend was not her current age may be because I *do* think of her as a childhood friend.

Having difficulty waking in several OOBEs vividly demonstrated my uncertainty as to which reality I was occupying - each reality was so real. I ultimately did find the correct reality and believe there must be some mechanism that assures that I do. The animal nature which changed from lizard to spider monkey to tiger could have been representative of Brian and me as brave creatures venturing into new territory. The changing form could also be one of the identifying properties of that particular dimension. The appearance of the Boy Scout signified to me, later of course, that help was near if I needed it. I was at that time still not aware enough OOB to recognize such symbolic aid.

OOBEs do not always follow physical laws. Bob's

instantaneous movement from our bedroom to Brian's is a vivid example of unusual dreamscape laws, abilities and characteristics. I do believe these laws will be apparent once enough people become conscious in, and investigate, the dreamscape/OOB reality. When we eventually compare data, patterns will emerge which will help us identify the parameters of OOB travel.

Full of Life

Many of my OOBEs had quite significant symbolic objects present in them. Upon analysis, when all I could see of my "unknown helper" were her hand and forearm, the analogy of the "hand of God" immediately came to mind. Not that I think it was the "hand of God," but that symbol, as well as the medicine bag, the fairies themselves, and the intensity of the OOBE lead me to believe the fairy OOBE was in actuality quite valid, if only emotionally. I have since learned that many features in tales of the Fey, their characteristics and that of their realm, are very similar to OOB experiences and encounters.

In the time-and-space OOB where I experienced elongated time in my normal body size and expanded space from the perspective of a micrometer body, notice the symbology of the red truck - a vehicle of transportation demonstrating unusual floating abilities. Then notice the unusual properties of time and space and the unique abilities of consciousness to transform itself. The whole theme of the OOBE revolved around unique OOB properties.

I also found it interesting that over six years later, 5-11-96, I found myself in very similar physical circumstances - looking down on my husband and a neighbor who looked remarkably like the man in the

OOBE. They were out in the front yard of our new residence, 800 miles away from where the OOBE originally occurred. My husband and neighbor weren't speaking of lawn sprinklers though they were where the lawn sprinklers existed - in the front yard. Time and space were again altered. This time I experienced the same events with the same people - only physically.

The OOBE in which I was experiencing other realities and couldn't seem to find the correct one is evocative of the illusory nature of perceived reality. If the parallel universe theory is correct and we are surrounded by identical realities encompassing all possible choices, then it seems to me our physical reality is just as illusive as the next. Only our belief in its permanence may keep us anchored to the habitually perceived patterns around us. Furthermore, *thought* was the necessary vehicle to enter the various realities I had experienced. I find it enticing that we can occupy a reality without being aware that it isn't physical reality. If we chose to inhabit a better world, would we automatically do so?

The headache I experienced when forcing myself out of my body was the only pain I ever encountered while OOB. In this OOBE and the one with all the loud noises, notice my following sound to reach the OOB state. I do this in many OOBEs and believe sound to be another vehicle to reach that state. Whatever form the sound may take, it is a Pied Piper to OOBEs.

Control

One of the major discoveries I made, which I am not claiming is original — but it was to me — was that consciousness moves into imagined images.

Functioning at all OOB with any sense of control only came after I learned to imagine myself sitting and walking. I would be places without the sense of having a body, so I didn't feel I controlled my journeys, or at least I didn't recognize that I did, until I felt I had a form.

Other beings, consciousnesses, appear to occupy inner space, and interaction is possible. This book shows a few instances where minor interaction occurred. The blue eyes and feminine voice were one instance. Who or what these people are is still open for debate.

Logical analysis and possibly memory access seem to be impaired when functioning in some OOB locations. This was particularly prevalent in the early OOB experiences I labeled as false-awakening dreams. Practice and more familiarity with the OOB environment appear to alleviate these problems.

Loss of energy OOB is interesting. The moving-dirt episode was one example. Do we only have so much energy with which to travel while OOB? And did my moving the dirt around the old sofa signify the sofa was now in some dump surrounded by dirt? The reality of the senses as they function OOB is indisputable despite the fact that these sensations come from a seemingly irrational experience.

The day I first experienced two prolonged OOBs was when extreme physical exhaustion reduced the amount of time it took to reach the OOB environment. The exhaustion usurped the normal difficulties of ignoring the physical body, which is imperative to OOB travel.

The OOB where I was speaking with relatives on the telephone and in person still flabbergasts me. It has been postulated that consciousness is quite mobile and can be in two places at once. This may have been what the telephone conversations signified. I do know that altered sleep patterns, the ability to focus, and shocking experiences were all tremendous aids in shifting my consciousness into alternate realities.

In *The Individual and The Nature of Mass Events* by Jane Roberts, Seth mentions that when mental patterns become strong enough, physical manifestations occur. Is this what happened with the Hueco Homes Realty manifestation? My answer, in the form of the telephone call, appeared at the exact time I was thinking of that OOB experience, didn't it? I think these synchronicities are reality creations, not merely significant coincidences. I believe we co-create these phenomena along with our Higher Selves as signposts of our creativity and abilities.

Progress

People have been OOB and met friends and relatives, though oftentimes the person met didn't recall the interaction. Meeting my son so frequently was in direct response to a thought of him. I didn't question him about my experiences. I felt he was too young to understand or to provide me with a valid answer. Given the multi-dimensional aspects of man, I believe some portion of Brian unconsciously was there with me, interacting with me and responding to my desire to be with him. His transformation into the harmless monster raises many questions. Until I can interact with someone OOB who knows they are OOB, I have no way of verifying if transformation of consciousness can be witnessed by an OOB traveler.

Travel OOB can be as fast or slow as you want it to be. When I went to the ocean, I wanted to experience flying sensations. Other times I just wanted to be somewhere. More controlled experiments with set times and destinations could yield fascinating information. As in the instance at the Gulf, this was an event/place that would occur, unknown to me at the time, in my future.

Who the robed figures were in one OOB, I still haven't discovered. One day I certainly hope to. When I walked through the gale and wondered about the future of our home, I appeared to be sifting through different probable scenarios of what could occur to the property. We do this constantly, of course, physically, choosing which event or path we wish to experience. OOB it just occurs in front of our eyes.

Hearing voices OOB and seeing figures make me wonder how solitary my excursions are OOB. Are there others present of whom I am not yet aware at a conscious level? The robed figures and voices indicate that this might be entirely possible.

Interaction

With much modern phenomena concerning extraterrestrials in circulation, the thought-form burglar comes to mind. Though I sincerely don't want to invalidate anyone's experience - we are unique individuals - I wonder how many such experiences are interactions in the OOB environment. This would not necessarily invalidate the experiences, but it might shine some light on the origin of these oftentimes fearful images.

Returning to my childhood home and encountering the White Light there spontaneously leads me to believe the White Light is a valid aspect of the OOBE. What it signifies is still unknown to me. I do find it interesting that when I wanted to go home, the White Light appeared spontaneously.

Seeing a past version of my mother was also very intriguing. Since I had met people from my future while OOB, it seems logical that I could also meet past versions of people.

I am aware that in most current literature regarding the OOBE, it is considered common knowledge that words viewed OOB can generally not be read. I have had this occur many times myself. But my Phantom experience demonstrates that this is not always so. Words can be read, but they will manifest into images or possibly strong emotions. If I hadn't had the evidence of the printed book, imagine my interpretation of that experience. (The Phantom experience occurred years before the now popular movie was on the market). That is why it is so important to be aware of your thoughts and to record everything you can remember. Details contain volumes of heretofore unknown information.

Past Associations

All of the phenomena trying to make me aware of the demise of my first husband revealed that we do live in some form after death. How long we remember or interact with the earth plane is nebulous. I do feel sorry for those who die with no knowledge of their true circumstances and abilities. Needless anguish might be alleviated by pre-death knowledge of thought-energy.

Hot Stuff

In my Demon OOBE, the demon was, I believe, a thought-form which resulted from my trying to remember the title of the Hot Stuff comic book. I also believe it was the result of the quote I read prior to leaving the bedroom and my thinking the drawing of the brain on the book jacket looked like a Rorschach test. In response to my unconscious memory of the text and that thought, I *was undergoing a test*. The test was one created to help me confront my fears and to recognize, in no uncertain terms, that I did not believe in demons. This OOBE gave me tremendous confidence that I could handle *anything* OOB as well, even one of the most feared mass creation myth symbols.

Introduction

In the introduction of this book, the Animator was a person with extremely interesting abilities. Though mental telepathy is the common mode of communication out of body, this entity was able to implant a powerful dynamic image in my mind, and I believe my mind to be inviolate to any intrusion from anything outside myself. No other consciousness I have encountered in my extensive OOB travels has had any power to control me or affect my consciousness in quite that manner. The Animator entity did.

For many years after this out-of-body experience, I considered the Animator to be a representation of my Higher Self. That part of me which breathes for me, that controls my unconscious functions, that provides the medium in which my life is based. Despite this fact, events have transpired which cause me to modify my initial assessment of the nature of the Animator.

When Bob, Brian and I first moved to a different part of the United States in 1996, I was totally surprised and disturbed to discover our new place to be similar to the OOB location in which the Animator appeared. Upon inspection, I felt that our new property *was* the exact location I had visited OOB.

When Bob and I first saw the property, we immediately fell in love with it. Abundant fruit trees, berry bushes, wild and domesticated roses, and other unique plants merged with the rest of the natural environment to capture our hearts. We were constantly delighted to discover unique plants growing on our property. No one was more surprised than I to recognize the similarity between the OOB landscape and the physical landscape.

An apple tree in our backyard so resembles the bread tree in my OOBE, that I am deeply moved every time I look at it. There just cannot be two trees that look so unbelievably alike. When gazing at the view from our backyard, each home has its own "hill," or part of one; each home has plenty of privacy in the countryside setting; and while looking in the direction where I had looked in my OOBE, I found a spot in our backyard where no homes are visible. In fact, I wonder if some of the houses weren't built after I visited the location in 1991 while OOB.

I was further surprised to discover the local town has a modern cobblestone outdoor shopping area with unfamiliar plants just like that in the OOB village. One section of the business community has a European feel and signs that faithfully mirror the quaintness of the OOB village. I was quite flabbergasted by the similarities until I came across a rational explanation.

Jane Roberts in her book *Psychic Politics: An Aspect Psychology Book* postulates - based on her own mystical experiences - that we each have inner living models upon which our physical forms and psychological patterns are based. These are not static models, but are ever changing *conscious* constructs from which we form our eccentric earth personality. Jane's experiences bore evidence that civilizations, cities and countrysides - all aspects of life - are built around similar gestalt models. This leads me to several conclusions.

The implanted image of the giant figure in the Animator OOBE, the Friendly Giant, was similar to other giant figures I have encountered before in my dream/OOB life. I believe these giant figures are symbolic representations of the higher aspects of our selves. I believe the Friendly Giant image was a representation of my inner model construct.

I do believe the bread tree and fruit in the OOBE were highly symbolic, and yet I know the physical apple tree is also quite validly an eccentric version of the OOB tree. Along these same lines, the local town appears to be an eccentric physical replica of the Animator OOB village. That is, the local landscape and the town are the physical versions of the combined psychological and probable sites I encountered OOB. The fact that within the OOBE the OOB location was an "ancestral" one makes me think it was a definite *future* "ancestral" association for me.

To say that I was awed by these discoveries is putting it mildly. I tried to deny what I was encountering at my new residence. But in the face of so much evidence, I cannot deny what I know to be true - even if it seems to defy all that we have been taught about reality. In the Animator OOBE, I traveled to a definite future space I was to occupy. I have no doubt that this is true. But there is more.

In the eccentric physical version of the OOBE reality, it was very difficult for me to agree with and come to terms with the similarities between the Animator and myself. I was five years younger when the Animator OOBE occurred. When I moved to our new home, I was gray-haired, much heavier, wore contacts lenses, and looked like the Animator. It wasn't until the property so mirrored the OOB location that I even noticed this fact. I tried to deny it because it seemed so incomprehensible - but finally I couldn't. **I had become a probable aspect of myself and had met that aspect OOB five years prior to when I would actually exist as that probable self.** And that probable self, me, had more abilities than I had in 1991... but that is another long story...

My journeys into the ubiquitous, magical out-of-body realm continue. I am constantly thrilled, shocked and awed. One thing I have learned from all of my experiences is that life is not what we have been taught. Life is much more magical and much more within our control and comprehension than we suspect. Our patterns of thought, our beliefs, and our intense desires dictate what we will experience, both in physical reality and out of it. We must think accordingly.

Epilogue

Trust the miracle of your own being.

Seth, *Mary Barton's Seth Quotation Quilt*

Well, miracles do never cease. The date is September 30, 2008. In the past couple of days, I was conducting research on the internet regarding a new business website, *In Tribute*, that I wanted to start. In my investigations, I came across an article that mentioned an internet book publishing company called *Lulu*. I noted it and didn't think much about it until last night when an airplane pilot and I were discussing our passions. This friend had recently launched a website revolving around his airplane flying passion, called *Wings of Men*. Although I was about to begin a new writing business myself, I knew that my true obsession, if I had the time to practice it, was out-of-body experiences. But life had intervened and curtailed that aspect of my existence for a number of years.

That night I didn't sleep well. I thought of my reasons for not pursuing, after initial attempts, the publication of this and several other books on the subject. Besides all of the complications associated with life, the main reason, I realized, was out of respect for my mother. She was a devout Roman Catholic, and I didn't want to embarrass her by my unorthodox experiences and beliefs. As she had passed away a little over a year ago, I knew there was no reason why I couldn't publish the books now. I had the time and I might bring hope to someone, somewhere, and add to the knowledge on the subject.

The next morning I awoke early, went straight to my laptop computer and looked up www.lulu.com. They did indeed publish books so I began to enter the information about this one in their database. When it occurred to me that I hadn't looked at *Soul Sight* in years, I decided to read it before I self-published. At 11:11am, I was stunned to have life wake me up once again.

Approximately twenty years ago I recorded the events that occurred in *Hot Stuff,* chapter twenty-eight, of this book. In the OOBE described, Brian and I were in a room with many books in it. **During the OOBE, I read the binding of one of the books which had *Lulu* imprinted on its spine—the *exact name* of the internet publishing company where I planned to publish *Soul Sight.*** Lulu is a company that has been in existence only since 2002. But it gets better.

My son is now 23-years-old, has a Bachelor of Science degree in Psychology, and is attending school to earn his doctorate in Cognitive Neuro-Science. When I recently talked to him, he mentioned that he had been working with computer brain scans for the first time to identify 'areas of interest' for his research. The OOB, if you remember, mentions that under the title of a book we were looking at, *Get Awake While You Can,* was the image of a human brain.

While author Richard Bach may have "told" me to write my book, this wondrous epiphany "told" me to publish it. I can only thank All That Is for renewing my faith, once again, in the undeniable magic of life.

End Notes

1. Page 120: Bach, Richard, *Illusions: The Adventures of a Reluctant Messiah*, (Delacorte Press/Eleanor Friede, 1977), p. 142.

2. Page 127: Hayward, Susan, *A Guide for the Advanced Soul: A Book of Insight*, (Crows Nest NSW 2065 Australia: In-Tune Books, 1985), p. 56.

Quotations

The Visitor: Jane Roberts, *Seth Speaks: The Eternal Validity of the Soul* (New York: Bantam Books), Session 539.

New Memory: Jane Roberts, *Seth Speaks: The Eternal Validity of the Soul* (New York: Bantam Books), Session 596.

Prediction: Jane Roberts, *Seth Speaks: The Eternal Validity of the Soul* (New York: Bantam Books), Appendix.

Symptoms: Jane Roberts, *Seth Speaks: The Eternal Validity of the Soul* (New York: Bantam Books), Appendix.

The Omega and the Alpha: Jane Roberts, *The Seth Material* (New York: Bantam Books), Chapter 13.

Discovery: Jane Roberts, *The Seth Material* (New York: Bantam Books), Chapter 10.

The Straw: Jane Roberts, *Seth Speaks: The Eternal Validity of the Soul* (New York: Bantam Books), Session 521.

Paradox: Jane Roberts, *The Unknown Reality, Vol. 1* (New York: Bantam Books), Session 684.

Memories: Jane Roberts, *The Unknown Reality, Vol. 1* (New York: Bantam Books), Session 684.

Dream Life: Jane Roberts, *Seth Speaks: The Eternal Validity of the Soul* (New York: Bantam Books), Session 531.

The Gift: Jane Roberts, *Seth Speaks: The Eternal Validity of the Soul* (New York: Bantam Books), Session 580.

Awakening: Jane Roberts, *The Seth Material* (New York: Bantam Books), Chapter 11.

Soul Sight: Jane Roberts, *Seth Speaks: The Eternal Validity of the Soul* (New York: Bantam Books), Session 575.

Flight: Jane Roberts, *Seth Speaks: The Eternal Validity of the Soul* (New York: Bantam Books), Session 538.

A Voice in the Night: Jane Roberts, *The Unknown Reality, Vol. 1* (New York: Bantam Books), Session 684.

Dimensions: Jane Roberts, *Seth Speaks: The Eternal Validity of the Soul* (New York: Bantam Books), Session 538.

Future Events: Jane Roberts, *Seth Speaks: The Eternal Validity of the Soul* (New York: Bantam Books), Session 566.

Getting Out: Jane Roberts, *The Unknown Reality, Vol. 1* (New York: Bantam Books), Session 683.

Loving: Jane Roberts, *Seth Speaks: The Eternal Validity of the Soul* (New York: Bantam Books), Appendix.

Energy Transfers: Jane Roberts, *Seth Speaks: The Eternal Validity of the Soul* (New York: Bantam Books), Session 572.

Lucidity: Jane Roberts, *Seth Speaks: The Eternal Validity of the Soul* (New York: Bantam Books), Chapter 11.

False Awakening: Jane Roberts, *The Unknown Reality, Vol. 1* (New York: Bantam Books), Session 700.

Full of Life: Jane Roberts, *The Unknown Reality, Vol. 1* (New York: Bantam Books), Session 701.

Control: Jane Roberts, *Seth Speaks: The Eternal Validity of the Soul* (New York: Bantam Books), Session 575.

Progress: Jane Roberts, *The Unknown Reality, Vol. 1* (New York: Bantam Books), Appendix 11.

Interaction: Jane Roberts, *The Unknown Reality, Vol. 1* (New York: Bantam Books), Session 700.

Past Associations: Jane Roberts, *Seth Speaks: The Eternal Validity of the Soul* (New York: Bantam Books), Session 540.

Hot Stuff: Jane Roberts, *Seth Speaks: The Eternal Validity of the Soul* (New York: Bantam Books), Session 587.

Conclusion: Jane Roberts, *Seth Speaks: The Eternal Validity of the Soul* (New York: Bantam Books), Session 580.

Epilogue: Seth, *Mary Barton's Seth Quotation Quilt.*

About the Author

Mary Barton has experienced and investigated out-of-body journeys since 1971. Although her innate talents emerged in childhood, in the years she actively investigated the phenomena, she experienced traveling into the future, into past reincarnational lives, and through physical space while out-of-body. Her subsequent interest in the topic led her to become a staff member for Seth Network International (SNI), an organization dedicated to the investigation of anomalous experiences in consciousness.

Barton was designated as a *Pioneer of Consciousness*, with subsequent story, in author Lynda Dahl's *Wizards of Consciousness*. She has participated in many lucid dreaming experiments, most notably with author Linda Lane Magallon, author of *Mutual Dreaming: When Two or More People Share the Same Dream*, and members of the *Fly-By-Night Club*. Her work has appeared in *Reality Change: The Global Seth Journal* and numerous other journals, newspapers, newsletters and magazines.

Barton is a former Product Manager for a publishing company, a former journalist and editor for two newspapers, a features editor and journalist for an industry magazine, a former Marketing Manager for a company that sells multi-million dollar motor homes, and a contract employee for one of the world's largest computer software companies. She received a B.S. from the University of Texas at El Paso, Texas in Computer Science. She currently resides in Kent, Washington where she is enthusiastically writing her subsequent books.

At SNI, she worked with Rob Butts, co-creator of the Seth Books; Lynda Dahl, author of *The Wizards of Consciousness, Ten Thousand Whispers*, and *Beyond the Winning Streak*; Susan M. Watkins, author of *Dreaming Myself, Dreaming a Town (Field Notes from the Land of Dreams)* and *Speaking of Jane Roberts: Remembering the Author of the Seth Material*; Norman Friedman, author of *The Hidden Domain: Home of the Quantum Wave Function (Nature's Creative Source)* and *Bridging Science and Spirit: Common Elements in David Bohm's Physics, the Perennial Philosophy and Seth*; Sheri Perl, author of *Healing From the Inside Out*; Nancy Ashley, author of *Create Your Own Dreams: A Seth Workbook* and Linda Lane Magallon, author of *Mutual Dreaming: When Two or More People Share the Same Dream*.